DIALECTICAL MATER

DIALECTICAL MATERIALISM

ASPECTS OF BRITISH SCULPTURE SINCE THE 1960S

Ridinghouse

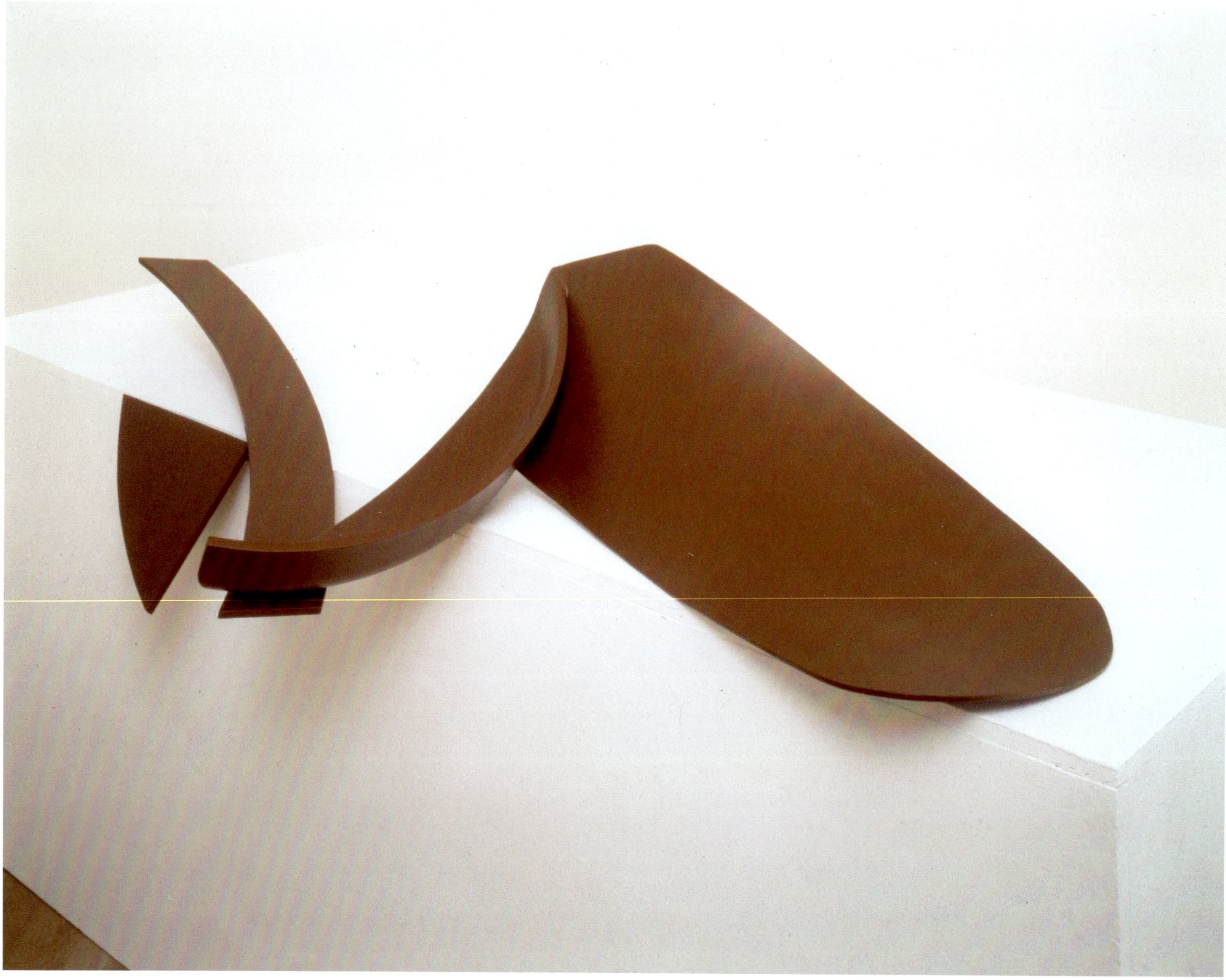

Anthony Caro, *Table Piece LXXVIII*, 1969
Steel painted matt brown, 44.5 × 154.9 × 57.2cm

CONTENTS

PREFACE

Tom Rowland, Director, Karsten Schubert Ltd

This exhibition is dedicated to Karsten Schubert, who died on 30 July of this year aged only 57. With great sadness, I write these few short words to honour him.

Karsten shared with all who knew him his profound love of art, his remarkable ability to create exhibitions that brought out the best in the work, and his delight in finding meaningful relationships between paintings or sculptures.

His collaborative aesthetic, his imagination and in particular his generosity – there are many artists who bear witness to this – will continue to inspire the team at Karsten Schubert Ltd. He lives on in the last exhibition he created but which he sadly did not see completed: his audaciously titled *Dialectical Materialism*, which brings together some of the most exceptional and ground-breaking sculptors of the last 100 years and is an immediate, tangible affirmation of his legacy.

I would like to thank Karsten for the many insights that he shared with us, and warmly express my gratitude to all the artists, gallerists and curators who have made this exhibition possible.

And after April, when May follows,
And the whitethroat builds, and all the swallows!
(Robert Browning, 'Home-Thoughts, from Abroad')

Karsten, we all miss you.

INTRODUCTION

Jon Wood

The story of British sculpture is often seen as one of generational rivalry and succession, in which groups of younger artists overthrow the ideas and objects of a previous generation. It is also, at the same time, seen as a story of continuity as well as of contestation; of absorption as well as reaction; of ongoing shared concerns as well as rupture; and as resulting in the renewal and revivification of sculpture more broadly.

Among its generational groups are the Young British Artists of the 1990s, the New British sculptors of the 1980s, the New Generation sculptors of the 1960s and the Geometry of Fear sculptors of the 1950s. This generation game of novelty, innovation and youth is often seen as a quasi-genealogical story of artistic lineages, art school educations and critical support, through the championing of dealers, writers, curators and institutional bodies. 'British sculpture' thus emerges as a construct that appears with resonance at distinct moments in time and within specific cultural contexts.

Dialectical Materialism: Aspects of British Sculpture since the 1960s, conceived by the late Karsten Schubert, is a bold, subtle and imaginative intervention into this complex subject, reconsidering its terrain through a small selection of artists and objects. In doing so, it focuses on objects more than contexts; on the artwork, not the art school. The title has two parts. The first part, 'Dialectical Materialism', a much debated term drawn from Marxist political philosophy, is deployed here to point to the dynamic and generative forces of opposition and reaction that have charged and driven the making of much sculpture in Britain since the postwar years. It also points to sculpture's place within a broader and technologically developing material culture. In the essay that follows, Jonathan Vernon looks into the potential of this concept in relation to the evolving treatment of materials, space and objecthood in British sculpture since 1960.

The second part, 'Aspects of British Sculpture', is drawn from Herbert Read's introduction to the catalogue for the British pavilion at the 26th Venice Biennale in 1952. In that text, which championed the work of Lynn Chadwick, Reg Butler, William Turnbull, Kenneth Armitage, Geoffrey Clarke, Bernard Meadows, Eduardo Paolozzi, Robert Adams and Henry Moore, Read coined the phrase the 'geometry of fear' to characterize these artists' curious, crab-like sculptures, which he imagined (through T. S. Eliot) 'scuttling across the floors of silent seas'.

It was a highly compelling phrase. Surrealist in spirit and existentialist in outlook, it captured the mood of the moment both sculpturally and culturally, pointing to a poetics of paradox and contradiction. 'Geometry', which we might associate with order, reason and beauty, is paired with 'fear' and the forces of chaos, anxiety and doubt. This present exhibition takes up the potentialities of juxtapositions such as this, exploring pairings and dialogues and celebrating the creative and highly productive tensions that can lie both between and within sculptural practices in this period.

The exhibition includes the work of six sculptors, to be seen both as a group and in dialogue with each other. They are: William Turnbull (1922–2012), Anthony Caro (1924–2013), Barry Flanagan (1941–2009), Richard Long (b. 1945), Alison Wilding (b. 1948) and Rachel Whiteread (b. 1963). Six large works – Turnbull's *Sculpture* (1956), Caro's *Andy* (1966), Flanagan's *metal 2 '64* (1964), Long's *Red Slate Circle* (1980), Wilding's *In a Dark Wood* (2012) and Whiteread's *Garage* (2005) – occupy the same ground both as each other and their inquisitive viewers, sharing in conversations and confrontations. Smaller works, more everyday in scale, have been placed on top of large tables, meeting the viewer at working hand height, offering up other aspects of comparison and a physical level of imaginative encounter.

This exhibition is thus an invitation to look back and forth between artists and objects, to reconsider connections and differences – some that sit more visibly on the surface and others that are more hidden and mischievous. It is an invitation to think about the shifting and dynamic deployments of natural and manmade materials and of processes such as carving, casting, modelling and construction. It is a chance to examine differing treatments of volume and line, of colour and surface, of weight and weightlessness, and of translucency and solidity, and to ruminate on the knowing shifts in conception and register that each of these artists employ. Alongside these aspects of tension and disjunction, surprising correspondences can be discerned between the sculptures on display, with moments of connection as well as contrast. Accordingly, this exhibition does not present a straightforward chronological survey; rather it presents six powerful large works that, by both taking centre stage and simultaneously operating as part of an ensemble, each stand for a sculptural position while also marking specific creative moments within the artists' wider oeuvres.

In keeping with the dialogical and comparative character of this exhibition, many of the works on display are themselves bipartite in form, suggesting conversations internal to the sculptures themselves. Through this, they also remind us of the haunting example of the 'mother and child' genre and of two-part composition more generally, much popularized by artists such as Henry Moore, highlighting the long, influential shadows cast by this motif and the artistic challenges and opportunities that the powerful double-form type offers. A two-part work is an immediate way of departing from the monolithic and from the single form enjoyed by so much statuary. It is also a means of introducing the psychically charged spaces of relationship, dialogue and distance between two entities. Such compositions, however they are articulated, are by nature highly generative; 1 + 1 = 3, you might say.

Dialectical Materialism: Aspects of British Sculpture since the 1960s is a subtle and thought-provoking exhibition that cuts into what is a huge subject through a closely edited selection of work, offering an intriguing cross-sectional slice through British sculpture's vibrant life, past and present. It can tell us many things, not only about these six important artists and their contribution to the field, but also, once in their company and sharing the same sculptural space, about the various ways in which we ourselves can reflect upon and reconsider our own changing relationship to the material world and the spatial environments that surround us.

DIALECTICAL MATERIALISM: ASPECTS OF BRITISH SCULPTURE SINCE THE 1960S

Jonathan Vernon

The Truth is the (W)hole

In 2008, the theorist Bill Livant arrived at a useful way of figuring perhaps the most important transition in dialectical thinking in the Western tradition: the shift from the Hegelian to the Marxist dialectic. For Hegel, Livant explains, the truth is the whole, the totality. For Marx, the truth is the hole, the hidden part that betrays the workings of a system. Marx's discovery was that we may only increase our understanding of the world by focusing our scrutiny on that which appears to us in the form of absence and inarticulacy – or, as Livant puts it, on 'the hole in Hegel's bagel'.[1]

'Hegel's bagel' is a neat pedagogic device. However, it is also an obviously sculptural idea, one that allows us to see much sculpture and sculptural thought of the twentieth century in a different light.

Sculpture is often framed in dialectical terms: it is an art of the inside and the outside, the hidden and disclosed, the part and the whole, essence and appearance. Such oppositions are superficially useful and convincing to us because they allow us to discern the order of a whole – a whole we call 'sculpture'.

What would it mean, then, to seek out the 'hole' of sculpture? It would mean treating as essential to sculpture that which appears not to be sculpture at all. It would mean, quite literally, treating the empty space around and within a sculpture as if it held the key to the object's meaning and being. It is only by considering space as belonging both to sculpture and to something else that it may attain the significance of Livant's 'hole' – that it may begin to disclose how sculpture really works. Space, within a sculptural environment, takes on a peculiar set of properties. Namely, it functions as a material, a medium shaped by sculptural activity, and as a world, a container in which to move and live and be. Not only do the viewer and the sculpture therefore share that same space, but the strange relations produced within it – perceptual, devotional, aesthetic – are fundamentally social, which is to say artificial and subject to change. The systemic character of sculpture, the true '(w)hole', is thus made legible.

To varying degrees, the sculpture of the past responded to and actively shaped the enchantment of space by social structures and procedures. It took on new forms within the temple, the church, the facade and the public square. With the onset of modernity, however, many of those structures and procedures were no longer sustainable, and the spells they cast over space were no longer convincing. The question of space – of whether space belonged to sculpture alone, to the viewer, or to some dangerous combination of the two – became a loaded one. In turn, sculpture began to see space differently, and to produce new kinds of relations.

British Sculpture since the 1960s

This exhibition includes the work of six sculptors: Anthony Caro, William Turnbull, Barry Flanagan, Richard Long, Alison Wilding and Rachel Whiteread. This essay will explore where these sculptors fit within a long historical moment, from the 1960s to the present, in which sculpture both sought to address itself to, and produced, new concepts of space.

Inevitably, a network of relations between these figures informs my analysis. All six of the sculptors are British, and they developed their practices against a backdrop of momentous change to the spaces in which sculpture was taught, funded, exhibited and legitimized. Anthony Caro, born two years after Turnbull, the oldest of the group, was an assistant to Henry Moore between 1951 and 1953. At this time, Moore's practice – monumental, public, scaled up and preoccupied with the human form – was evolving into a paradigm against which younger British sculptors, including Caro, would soon have cause to rebel.[2] By the 1980s, when Rachel Whiteread, the youngest sculptor examined here, arrived on the national scene, the Henry Moore Foundation was awarding sculpture grants that utterly transformed the prospects of artists working in the medium. Although Whiteread worked as an assistant to Wilding as Caro once had for Moore, opportunities to gain experience were far greater in number and more widely accessible.

Beginning in the 1960s, art schools had become powerful spaces of inclusivity, interdisciplinarity and alternative thought, often representing the first port of call for young working-class adults seeking new social and cultural experiences, enabled by grants from the state. This process was accelerated at the close of the 1960s by the absorption of many art schools into Polytechnics – one product of which, the Faculty of Art and Design at Brighton Polytechnic, gave Whiteread her start. This was a far cry from the sculpture course at Saint Martin's School of Art in the early 1960s, headed by Frank Martin and taught by Caro – a non-hierarchical, practice-led learning environment, but one fiercely concentrated on sculpture as an independent discipline and populated chiefly by privately educated children of the British Empire.[3] As early as the mid-1960s – when Flanagan and Long attended Saint Martin's – the school was expanding its intake, and its narrow definition of sculpture was soon to be contested from within.[4]

Sketched out in this way, the story of British sculpture from the 1960s to the present becomes one of expansion. The definition of sculpture opened outwards, from the closed forms of figure sculpture in the 1950s to the open, unbounded sculptural installations, technical experiments and multimedia work of the late 1960s onwards. Educational and exhibition spaces multiplied and opened their doors to a more diverse public, spawning new kinds of sculptors and viewers alike. Guided principally by the works themselves, this essay tells a different story: the story of a sculpture that perceived within the necessity of expansion the threat of its own dissolution; a sculpture that maintained an acute feeling for the object, while understanding that the waning modernist tradition had proven it to be insufficient; and a sculpture that repeatedly figured these contradictions and the anxieties born out of them through its relations to space.

Sculpture/Object

The changes in British sculpture wrought by Anthony Caro at the beginning of the 1960s are invariably traced to his 1959 visit to the United States. During this visit he spent time with a number of Abstract Expressionist painters, the sculptor David Smith and the modernist critic Clement Greenberg, who had visited Caro's studio earlier that year. Upon his return, Caro began working on painted, welded steel sculptures placed directly on the ground, such as *Early One Morning* (1962). Caro's new sculptural idiom was linear; it possessed real weight while seeming to defy gravity, the heaviness of the steel belied by welded joints and vibrant colour; and its abstraction was lyrical, combining arabesques, flat planes and the insistent push–pull of the horizontal and vertical. For a critic like Greenberg, it was easy to see this idiom as a direct extension not only of Smith's project, but of a European modernist tradition that flowed from Pablo Picasso's constructions through Vladimir Tatlin's reliefs, Constantin Brancusi's 'pictorial, graphic' language of forms,[5] and Julio González's 'drawing in space'. As such, Caro provided further validation of Greenberg's belief that, unlike modern painting, the sculpture of the age had not evinced an internal drive towards 'medium specificity' but, rather, had 'turned out to be almost as exclusively visual in its essence as painting itself'.[6]

How, we might ask, can a sculpture so described also be seen as part of a tradition that recognized space for what it is – that saw disenchanted, everyday space as inseparable from sculpture's identity? The unsurprising answer is that Greenberg's assessment of Caro, as well as the more concerted (but nonetheless reverential) analysis of Greenberg's acolyte Michael Fried,[7] was inaccurate. Caro had not succeeded in severing sculptural forms from the world of everyday things, but rather sublimated their tendency to signify. How this sublimation functioned was quite different from the multivalence of Picasso's constructions and assemblages, which had always thrived on metaphor – on the bicycle seat of *Bull's Head* (1942), for example, signifying as a bicycle seat and a bull's head all at once. Indeed, only rarely do Caro's sculptures include anything truly legible as a 'sign'. Rather, his steel beams come close enough to not signifying at all

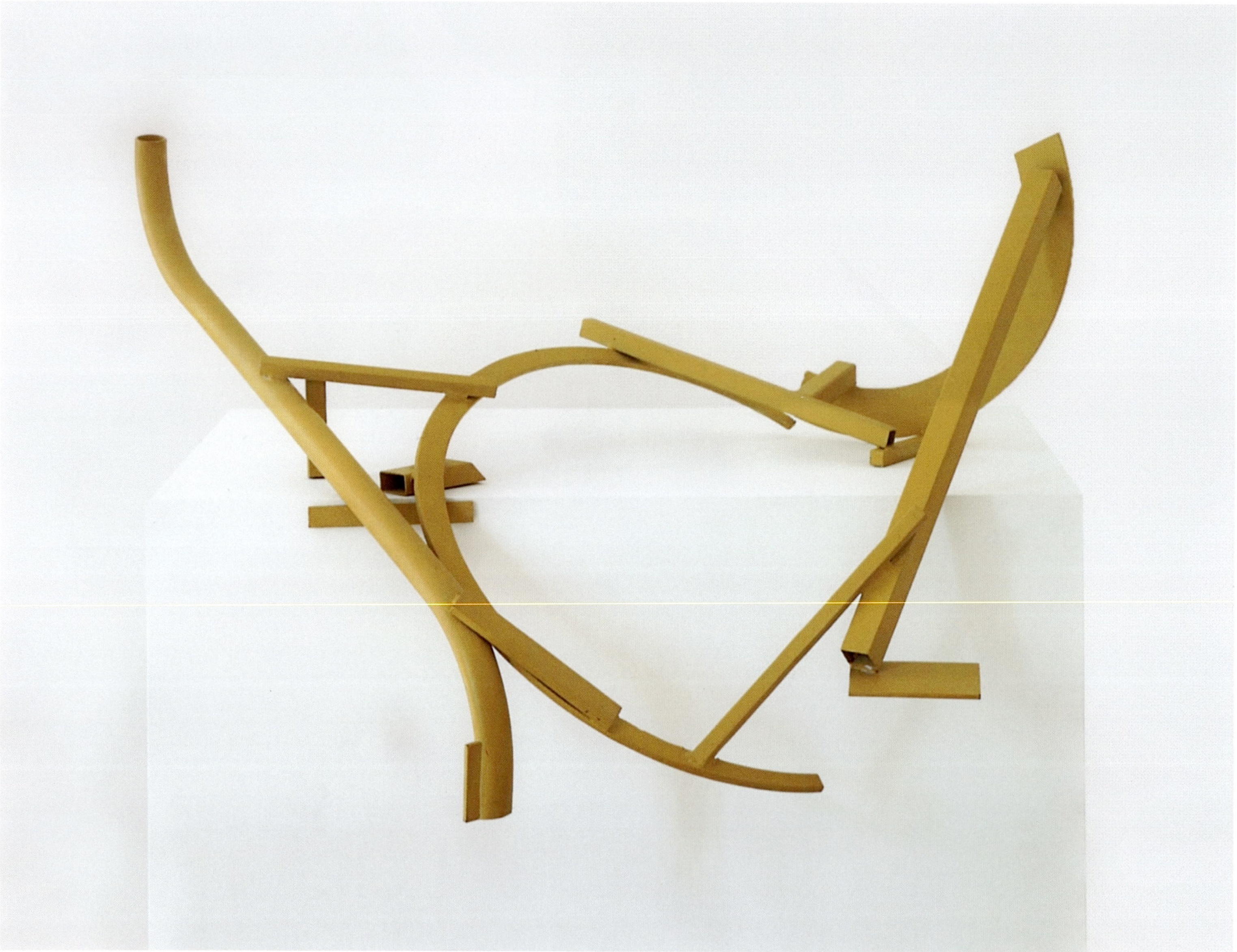

Fig.1. Anthony Caro, *Table Piece LXIV (The Clock)*, 1968
Painted steel, 76.2 × 132.1 × 81.2cm, private collection

that they become indeterminate, open-ended spaces of allusion. As Alex Potts puts it, 'Caro's most intriguing work is poised on a tightrope. For all its radical abstraction, vestiges nevertheless persist of figurative reference and mimetic realism.'[8]

Of course, these vestiges do not themselves prove that Caro acknowledged the literal character of sculptural space. But they do point up a common trait of the sculptures examined in this essay: that space frequently enters through, and its strange character is frequently disclosed in, the territory where sculpture and the quotidian object meet.[9] Nowhere in Caro's work is this more palpable than in his Table Pieces, such as *Table Piece LXIV – The Clock* (1968; fig.1), a sculpture once owned by Greenberg. Scaled to and placed on raised surfaces, or 'tables',[10] their size and composition tend to produce a resonance with the object-form of everyday things, sometimes going so far as to incorporate found objects. Positioned at the edge of the 'table', and typically spilling over it, these sculptures not only function as images but have a sense of being graspable, inviting touch. At the same time, this sense is often frustrated by the manifest uselessness of the object, or by the ungainly nature of the parts that stretch out into our space.

There are two kinds of liminality at work here. The Table Pieces operate not only in a space between abstraction and mimesis, but between opticality and tactility. Viewed as a testing ground, the Table Pieces may be seen as studies in how the modernist sculpture-object secures its autonomy – that is, in tension with its implicit constraints, the incessant presence of the horizontal and the vertical, the floor and the wall. In accepting these constraints as their subject, they necessarily resonate with the character of embodied, everyday human experience. They signify as part of our world by reaching out into our space, even as they frustrate the urge to reach back – like the handle of a knife trespassing over the edge of a table in a still-life by Cézanne. We may still be looking into a space of illusion, but the borders between that space and our own have declared themselves to be contestable.

This understanding of Caro's work points up a surprising affinity with the contemporary sculptures of William Turnbull. When in 1981 Lynne Cooke sought a useful means of categorising British sculpture of the 1960s, she divided it into the 'pure' abstraction of the New Generation sculptors who emerged under Caro's tutelage at Saint Martin's and the 'reformers' of modern European sculpture, headed by Turnbull, Eduardo Paolozzi and Hubert Dalwood.
As Cooke explains, the reformers worked to construct 'a morphology of simple monolithic shapes', drawn and adapted from modernist, ancient and non-Western precedents.[11] The most important of those precedents was Brancusi, whose vocabulary of stacked and carved forms in wood, stone and bronze was especially visible in Turnbull's sculpture from around 1958 until the mid-1960s.

Far from mere mimicry, Turnbull's appropriation of Brancusi's sculptural language followed a highly selective process, one especially focused on the grammar of that language and a class of forms within it that could be described neither as 'ornamental' nor mimetic. The result of this process was a world of forms with anthropomorphic resonance that nevertheless lacked any markers that might identify them as part of our – or indeed any – world. In short, Turnbull was using Brancusi's object-language to speak in 'potent if vague metaphor' – a trait that Cooke identified as fundamental to the project of the 'reformers', but which was equally critical to Caro's sculpture, as we have seen.[12]

Far from an isolated exercise, the parameters of Turnbull's project in the late 1950s and early 1960s can be seen to have directly informed what followed when, around 1963, the sculptor turned his hand to steel. Unlike Caro, Turnbull did not take advantage of the strength of the material, nor its suitedness to large, open constructions. Just as his works in bronze, stone and wood tended towards elemental forms and unmodulated surfaces, his pieces of steel showed few signs, but for their placement and dimensions, of the sculptor's intervention. As Patrick Elliott has remarked, the resulting sculptures 'are perceptual rather than conceptual or theoretical works, acting on the viewer in a direct way . . . Through minimal manipulation Turnbull transformed banal materials into new kinds of experiences.'[13] The nature of those experiences is laid bare by *Sextet* (1966; fig.2), which consists of six discrete objects, each made up of three welded steel beams marking out three edges of a cube. However, the six variations are designed to be moveable, and thus to change both the space in which they are shown and the viewer's pathway through that space, in an almost infinite number of permutations. Sculpture had moved off the plinth and into our space, and could now court an almost total abstraction while remaining unmistakeably about us – our ways of thinking, seeing and being within space.

Something is Wrong

In 1972, Barry Flanagan sent out an invitation to an exhibition of his work at Rowan Gallery, London. Printed on the invitation was a photograph of Flanagan, looking impassive in a mask and bowler hat, reflected in the mirror of *Sixties' Dish* (1970; fig.3). This work consisted of a sofa pushed flush to a wall-mounted mirror, with a cello nestled in the seat. It stood apart from the mainline of Flanagan's production that he had developed since attending Saint Martin's in 1964–65, largely in tension with the school's narrow definition of sculpture.

During this period, shape had been perhaps the central and most fiercely argued concern at the School. Flanagan's tutor Phillip King, one of several

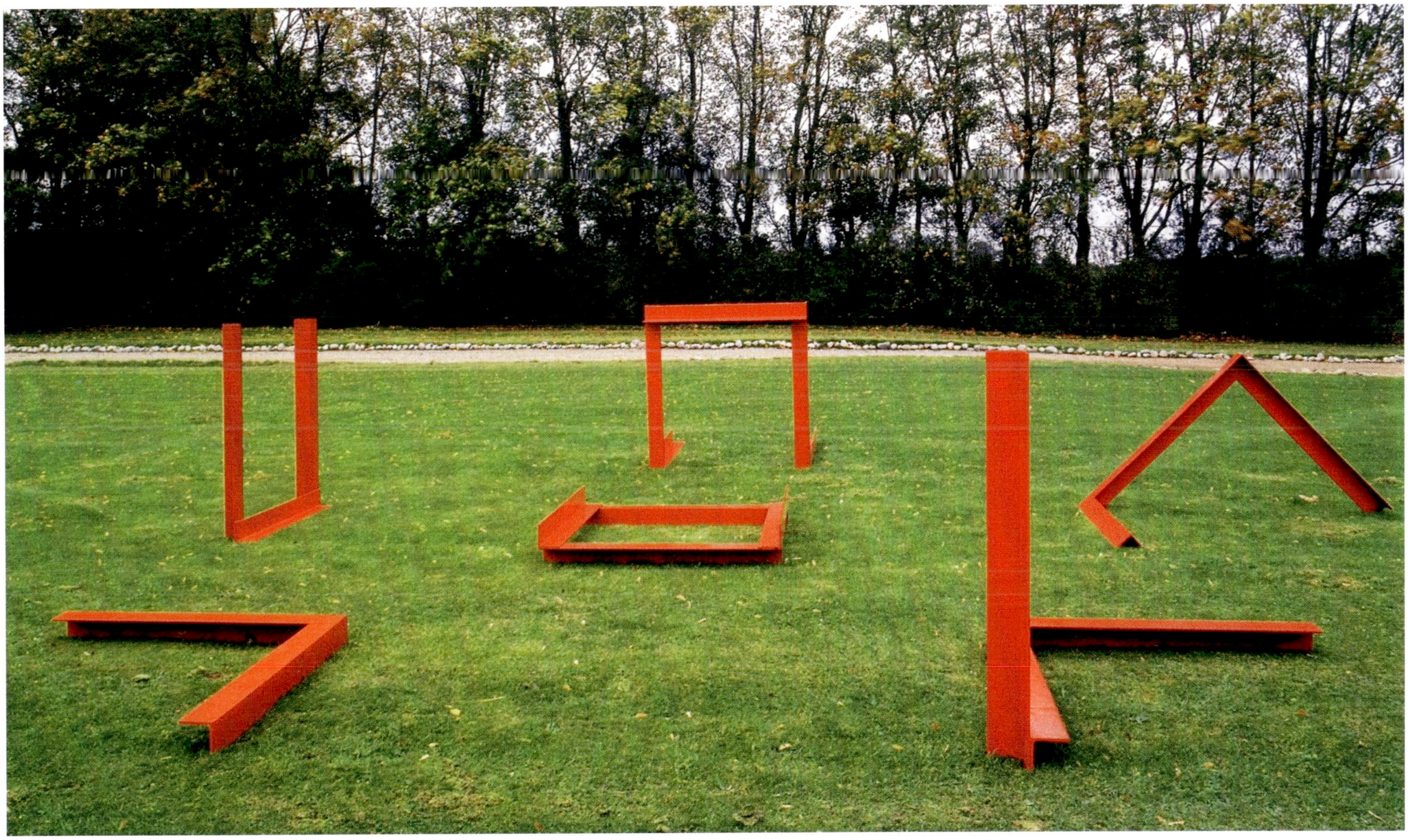

Fig.2. William Turnbull, *Sextet*, 1966–67
Painted steel, six elements each measuring 137.2 × 12.7 × 12.7cm
Waddington Custot, London

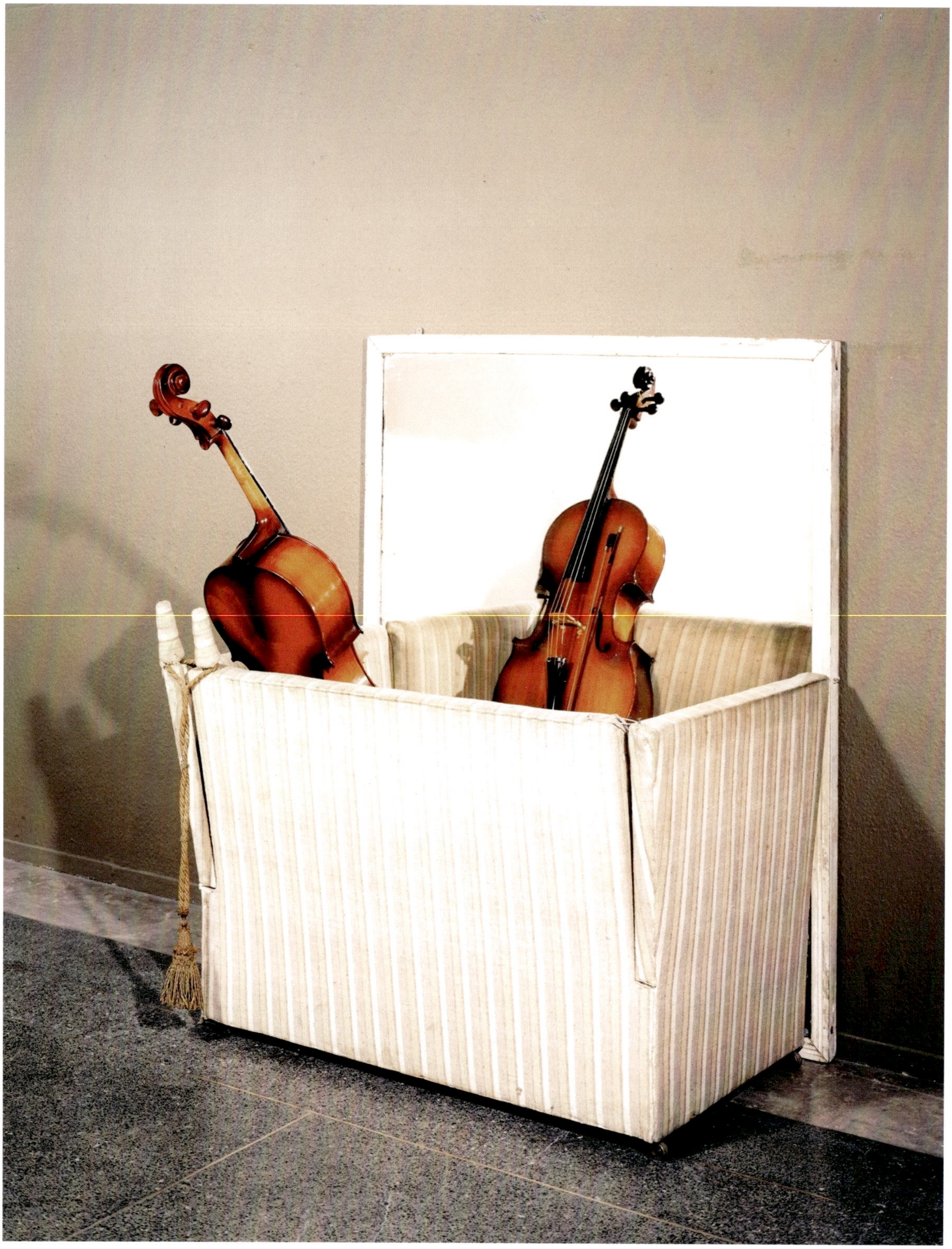

Fig.3. Barry Flanagan, *Sixties' Dish*, 1970
Glass, cello, bow and sofa, 157.5 × 134.6 × 95.2cm, Tate, London

former students who took over that year while Caro was in America, had set about exploring the formal possibilities of the cone (see *Through*, 1965; fig.4). In response to this elemental language, Flanagan had begun to work towards a poetic, worldly vernacular. But *Sixties' Dish* spoke in a different tongue. It exhibited no clear interest in materials, their tactility or their transformation. It had no place within the 'visual Thesaurus' Flanagan had mapped out through the use of taxonomical titles (such as *ringn '66* (1966), denoting 'ring, noun, 1966'),[14] and nor did it seem to allow much room for chance and interpretation in its installation, as did the loose configurations of ropes and sandbags that made up his early sculptural installations. What most tied the sculpture to what had come before was an inscription on the painted frame of the mirror, reading: 'JOHN THIS MIRROR TO STAY HERE NOT FOR [blank] P.M.' Language had always been critical to the signifying processes of Flanagan's work, but, even in this, *Sixties' Dish* was different. In 1974, Flanagan would assert that 'the mirror was acquired with my wife's house in Camden 4 years ago. (The inscription is only significant as a claim of ownership to prevent the demolition team removing it when they began work).'[15] Here was an artist providing context for his work to invalidate the contextual clues literally inscribed onto its surface; an artist addressing a message exclusively to a named, but absent, individual in a work addressed to an unknown, but present, viewer; an artist explaining his intentions to negate his intentionality.

Sixties' Dish introduces something to the narrative of sculpture in this period – a period of transition that says so much about what came before and after – that cannot easily be retracted. In describing the precise nature of that something, it is difficult to improve upon the words of Tim Hilton: 'The theme is domestic, aesthetic and negative . . . one has the sensation that something has gone wrong and that Flanagan is sparing us by touching on the matter lightly or tangentially.'[16] Hilton is suggesting that the effect of this work rests on an undisclosed or incomplete narrative, the sum of the 'domestic, aesthetic and negative' coming together and failing to signify. Whereas Caro and Turnbull had set the historical, tactile and everyday associations of the sculpture-object loose through abstraction, Flanagan seemed to have a specific referent in mind, from which he then turned away. But this is not the full story, since the component parts of *Sixties' Dish*, the cello, couch and mirror, also conspire in a carefully directed play of false allusions, doublings and inversions. By dismissing the meaning of the inscription on the frame of the mirror, Flanagan does not surrender authorship, but defers it – since the dismissal is itself a performative extension of the author-function. 'The inscription is only significant as a claim of ownership' – which is to say that it is a kind of signature. What has happened here? The spaces in which we live have been displaced, become distant and maybe hostile. Those from which we draw meanings and

Fig.4. Phillip King, *Through*, 1965
Plastic, 213 × 335 × 274cm, edition of three
Thomas Dane Gallery, London

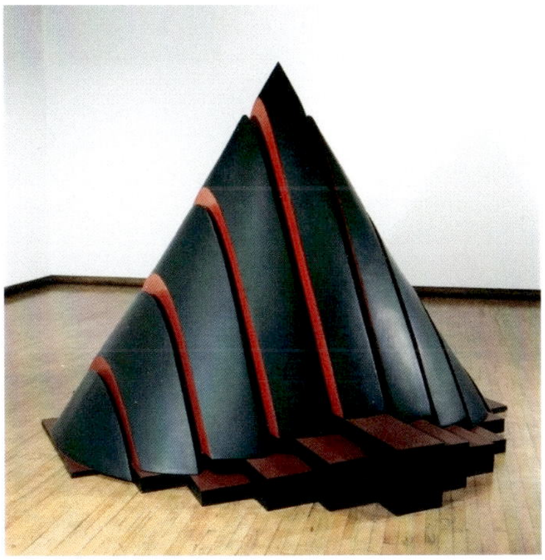

values, the spaces of illusion, have become so close as to be illegible. Something has gone wrong.

Flanagan's work acts out a particularly strange negation of the modernist sculptural paradigm. This is not a negation of substitution, replacing one thing with another. Rather, it is a negation that performs the latent contradictions and oppositions in something heretofore articulated as irreducibly whole – locating one thing within the other, and thereby transforming them both. In the case of *Sixties' Dish*, the 'things' in question are the 'illusory' and 'real' spaces of art and everyday life. In order to understand the broader implications of this manoeuvre, we may see Flanagan's negation of the conventions of modern sculpture as an echo of Raymond Williams's intervention in the prevailing currents of Marxist thought in the 1960s and 1970s, specifically through his concept of 'structures of feeling'.[17] Understood as a new solution to the old Marxist problem of reconciling theory and praxis, 'structures of feeling' emphasized the role of affect in determining the organization of social life, shaping what we believe, how we communicate and how we (quite literally) see the world. This was not to dispense *tout court* with the traditional attachment of Western philosophy to the world-making capacity of ideas. Rather, it was to insist that the ideas that structure our world are not independent of our experience of the world, and that, in turn, the emotional content of our experience is not to be dismissed as subjective and unanalysable. As Williams notes, this is 'not feeling against thought, but thought as felt and feeling as thought: practical consciousness of a present kind, in a living and interrelating continuity'.[18]

It seems to me that Williams's description maps perfectly onto the experience of seeing a sculpture by Flanagan. So often in his work, the apprehension of rational organization and the recognition of some deeply articulate but scarcely explicable feeling are simultaneous and indivisible. In the case of *Sixties' Dish*, we experience this simultaneity through a form of self-negation, a frustration of our ingrained tendencies as thinkers, readers, viewers and bodies that brings each of these functions dangerously close to one another. But, as should already be clear, I also think that the symbiosis of thought and feeling described by Williams corresponds to a far broader sense of what sculpture was doing from the late 1960s onwards, a sense uniquely inscribed in the work of the six artists studied here. For now, it is enough to say that sculpture was moving back into the space of the subject, the viewer; that it was doing so through perverse self-limitation on the one hand, and seemingly desperate extensions of the strategies historically available to it on the other; and that the failure of these efforts was in effect the cost of the medium retaining its identity.

Possessions

As Flanagan's work has shown, the evocation of domestic space – a space we know, share and might inhabit – opens up a number of avenues to sculpture. It might be imagined that the spaces of the home are where the everyday finds its essential character, in clutter and kitsch; that insofar as these spaces obtain a constant shape they also recede into the periphery, flimsy backdrops for events that serve only to lend an illusory structure to the passage of time. In fact, the physical spaces of the home are clearly contiguous with and shaped by structures of feeling.

Rachel Whiteread has made a study of the enchantment of domestic spaces. The sculptures that made her name, *Ghost* (1990) and *House* (1993), are so much about the dialectic between lived experience and living space, and the traces left in one by the other. But here, too, something is wrong. As with *Sixties' Dish*, the viewer is locked out of a space designed to house them. More than that, in having been cast and made concrete, the space still refuses to yield to the disinterested gaze of one wholly, safely on the outside. The scale of the cast denies that gaze – we are always too close, an experience well captured by the artist's experience of having 'become the wall' when she viewed the work after its completion.[19] In this, *Ghost* in particular illustrates what has always been true of the minimal object at its most affecting. That is, it is a wall, a floor, a room, scaled to the human body, and not a pair of disembodied eyes floating in space. The critical difference between Whiteread's architectural-scale casts and the minimal object is also a master key, I think, to her language. A Carl Andre floor piece appeals to the *condition* of floor-ness, and may be stood upon without becoming itself a floor. *Ghost* insists that it is not just a room, but *this* room – and in the same breath declares that room to be absent.

It may seem that all of this amounts to saying that Whiteread's sculptures are casts – a point surely not in need of labouring. The question is, what kinds of casts? Rosalind Krauss's answer is that they are death masks – afterimages of life, but also sites in which to play out death in the absence of any rituals or beliefs compelling enough to integrate death into the symbolic structures of modern society. Krauss defines these sites as 'entropic' and 'asymbolic', following Roland Barthes' discourse on the photograph as death mask in *Camera Lucida*.[20] This is not to say that Whiteread's casts have no symbolic structure of their own, but that 'they are signposts pointing elsewhere, to an elsewhere before the object'.[21] The way Whiteread's work articulates absence, and the nature of the absence being articulated, is a little more complex than Krauss's characterization allows, however. This has much to do with the fact that Whiteread's casts of architectural space are invariably seen as the apotheosis of her practice – when they in fact show that practice marking out its territory.

Whiteread's smaller-scale works – the bookshelves, water bottles, light switches and furniture – have a distinct object-language. They are cast in coloured resins, various metals, rubber, concrete and plaster. They include positive as well as negative casts. They engage with the cast's traditional association with the multiple and serial variation, whereas her architectural casts are invariably singular and typically site-specific. In other words, they amount to a far more differentiated exercise, one that exacerbates the conflict at the heart of the cast-as-object. The cast is, per Krauss, akin to the photograph in that it acts out a kind of death, a reification of something 'from life'. And yet however much the casting process lends itself to the reproduction of the reified image, it also produces objects with a distinct material identity. This aspect of Whiteread's work, as Briony Fer recognizes, also gives it a purchase in the present. 'The work may not appeal to newness, but neither is it necessarily "old". Rather, it seems of uncertain age, and most of all, susceptible to time.'[22] As Fer also notes, this has to do with materials above all. Whiteread's resin casts are permeated with light. Her plasters may evoke in the same breath the storerooms of the academy and the walls of the modern gallery. The object points elsewhere, but its motion is restless – and in its domesticity, whether the effect is of intimacy or alienation, it cannot help but point to ourselves.

What this gesture might signify, and how it might relate to the self-negation of *Sixties' Dish*, is well illustrated by Whiteread's *WAIT* (2005; fig.5). It comprises an unremarkable wooden chair and a number of plaster boxes stacked on and beneath it. The first point of reference suggested by the sculpture – one never far from Whiteread's thinking – is Bruce Nauman's *A Cast of the Space under My Chair* (1965). And yet the internal logic of *WAIT* is as far removed from Nauman's cast as Whiteread ever gets. The stack of boxes beneath the chair is orderly, but imperfect; its relation to the space it occupies is approximate. The chair itself is part container, part pedestal, fundamentally unlike and only provisionally connected to the objects it holds.

This radically non-identical relationship between parts is, of course, similar to that of *Sixties' Dish*. It conjures a familiar situation inexplicably arrested in time and thus rendered strange, taking the form of a constellation of things. The common property of these things in *Sixties' Dish* and Whiteread's work corresponds to what Heidegger called the 'ready-to-hand': the way in which certain objects, like tools, seem to exist for us only as part of a system of practices, and thus fail to register as things-in-themselves (a state which the tool-like protrusions of Caro's Table Pieces also clearly evoke).[23] The shape of our world, and the shapes into which it forces our experience, may be discerned most clearly in these objects. By making her objects part of a feasible, 'lived' scenario suspended in time, Whiteread pulls them to the surface. In doing so, she produces not only an iconography of domestic space, but a truly negative

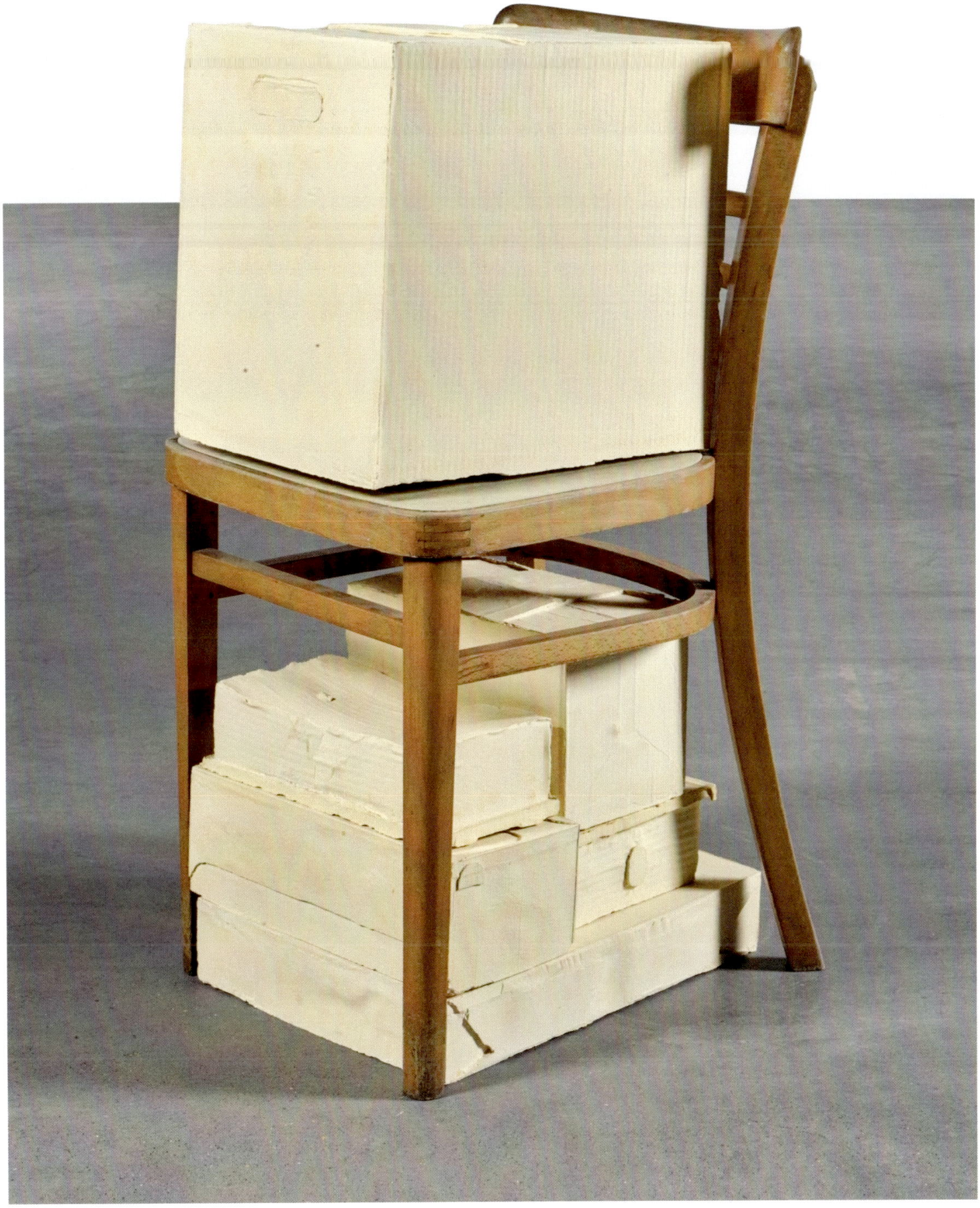

Fig.5. Rachel Whiteread, *WAIT*, 2005
Plaster and wood, 79 × 39 × 41cm, private collection

image of that space. To put it another way, the 'elsewhere' to which Whiteread's sculpture points is also an everywhere, happening all at once, in which we live without knowing it. The paradox is that we may not come to know it, since Whiteread can only present it to us in excerpts, and thus distortions – as sculptures, and never quite as objects. In this sense, Krauss's point, and the underlying pessimism of her semiotics, retains a kind of truth – we are no closer to the absent thing for having seen the space where it should be. And yet, we may come to *feel* it.

Marks on the Ground

A profound sense of the relationship between sculptural and everyday space as it is outlined in this essay is captured by the 'oblique' mode of address that Briony Fer has attributed to the small sculptures of Alison Wilding. Fer locates a specific kind of 'wrongness' in Wilding's sculptures, one generated by their object-like reticence and simultaneous lack of an object-form that would identify them with the world as we know it: 'it is hard', Fer says, 'to say what they *are*.' Fer is careful to set this idea of wrongness apart from surrealist metaphor, identifying it instead with 'the more mobile and multiple metonymy, the slippages between things that move from part to part'.[24] How this mode of address relates to space makes all too clear its relationship to the narrative of sculpture I am attempting to delineate here. As Fer writes, '[Wilding's] work . . . retains its distinctness as sculpture. But even as I say this, it seems even more pressing to clarify that what is distinct about sculpture has been radically transformed in Wilding's work to incorporate and activate the space around it.'[25]

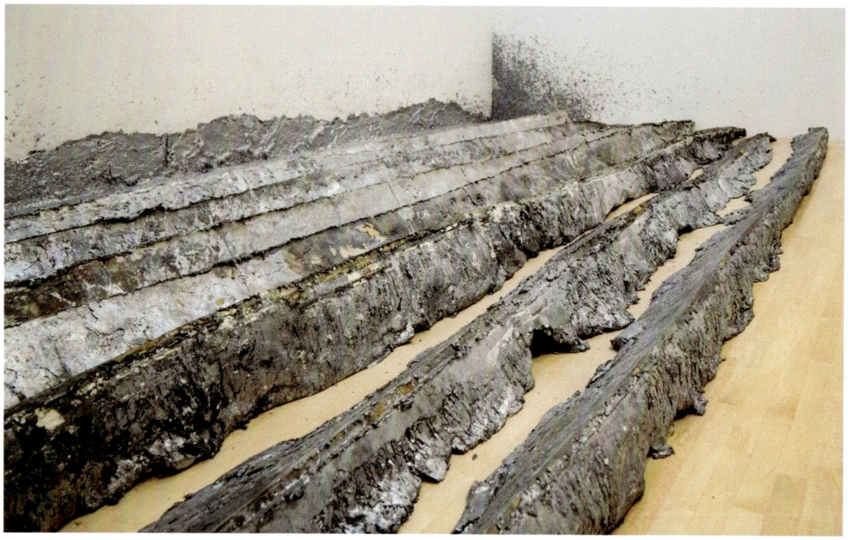

Fig.7. Richard Serra, *Gutter Corner Splash: Night Shift*, 1969/1995
Lead, 48.3 × 274.3 × 454.7cm, San Francisco Museum of Modern Art

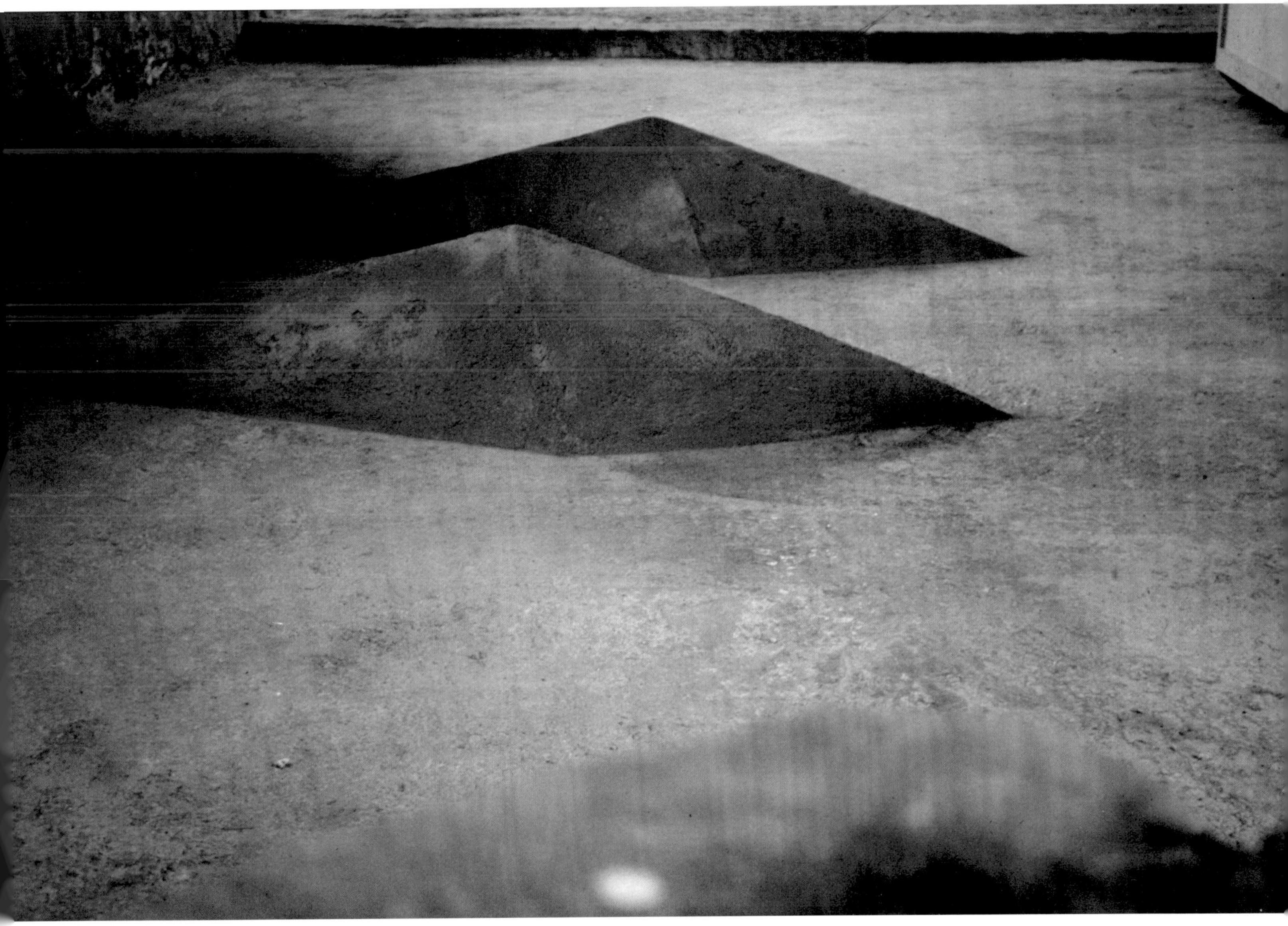

Fig.6. Alison Wilding, *In Shadow*, 1998
Rendered concrete, two objects, each 38 × 255 × 86cm, installed and photographed in the Chapel of St John the Evangelist, Skipton Castle, Yorkshire; destroyed

In Wilding's larger sculptures, this incorporation and activation of space operates through another kind of wrongness: a sense of threat, of a trap set for the viewer. Jo Applin cites a diary entry written by Wilding in 1976, titled 'Suspicion of Objects', as fundamental to understanding this idea. Contrasting 'Suspicion of Objects' to Richard Serra's famous 'verb list' of 1967, an index of physical sculptural processes, Applin suggests that Wilding's text 'reads instead as though it was a series of cautionary warnings'.[26] The first part of the text – 'On viewing / On tripping / On watching / On leaving' – seems almost a thesis statement for the much later, site-specific concrete work *In Shadow* (1998; fig.6).[27] Installed within the chapel of St John the Evangelist at Skipton Castle, North Yorkshire, *In Shadow* seems to obliquely reference the low forms of tomb effigies while taking the disenchantment of the traditional spaces in which sculpture was seen and understood to its logical conclusion. It insists that within this space a certain kind of conflict is being played out. The space around *In Shadow*, unlike that of Serra's molten lead works (fig.7), is not only one in which we move and live, but one in which we may be harmed if we are not attentive to its true nature, and the snares that lie within it.

Applin goes on to highlight the anthropologist Alfred Gell's observation that traps illustrate the false dichotomy between art and the artefact, aesthetics and function. Like works of art, Gell argues, traps initiate a mediated encounter between two beings in space and time that will at least change, and perhaps compromise, the condition of one or the other party.[28] The work of the final artist to be considered here, Richard Long, does not carry the air of threat implied by this analogy. It approaches the natural world and the social beings that move through it in a way that is measured, sensitive, and even, in Fer's sense, oblique. But it is substantially concerned with the forms taken by our occupation of that world, and the encounters we stage within it. This was recognized even in the earliest analyses of his practice; as Marina Vaizey put it in 1970, 'Richard Long's work is concerned with the interaction of man and landscape, not in the usual conventional sense of man as farmer, man as settler, but man acting out ritual; and leaving in fields of grass or in miles of desert, marks related to magic, and religion.'[29] The example Vaizey cites is *Inca Rock, Campfire Ash* (1972; fig.8), a juxtaposition of two photographs: a zig-zag form made by Long out of campfire ash, and a megalithic structure at Lake Titicaca (now thought to have functioned as a solar calendar and to have pre-dated the Inca). The relationship between these two images is, from a rational standpoint, unclear. But it is profoundly felt. These are the attempts, equally ancient in sentiment, of humans to use sculptural form to orient themselves within the world – not so much carving a space within it as delineating a space that already exists. Testament to this is provided by Long's own set of verbs, quite distinct from Applin's or Serra's and provided by another early review, by Richard Cork.

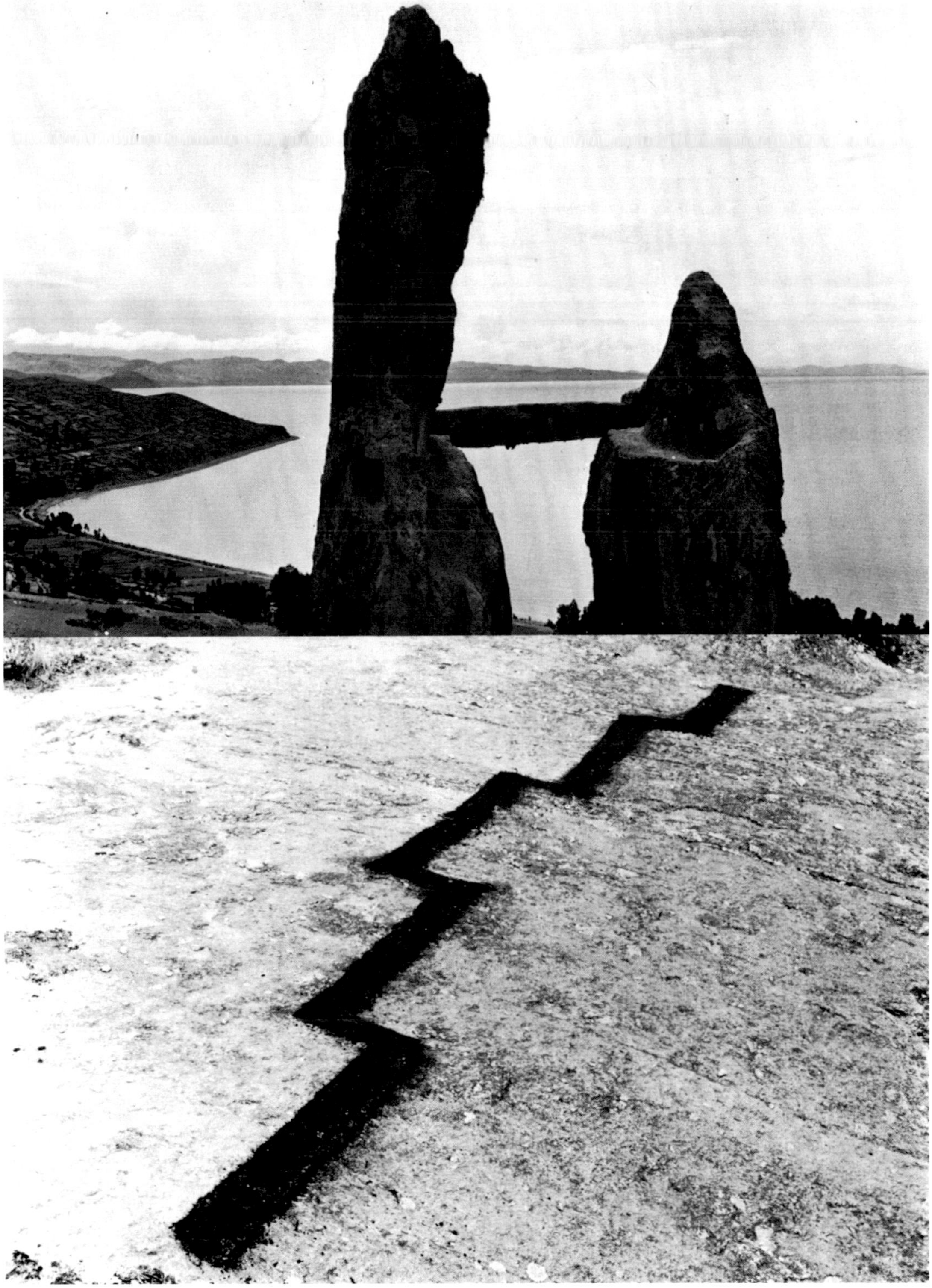

Fig.8. Richard Long, *Inca Rock Campfire Ash*, 1972
Black-and-white photograph, 86.9 × 64cm, private collection

Long is 'treading, subtracting, disclosing, sifting, trailing, supplementing, pointing, touching, laying, imparting'.[30] It might be that the space coaxed into being through such verbs, palpable still in the distant spaces of the world traversed by Long, is what each of the sculptors studied here was working towards. It might be that the 'wrongness' that became so fundamental to their different projects was a result of trying to bring such a space into our own.

Postscript

By locating within this body of sculpture a set of aesthetically radical terms (if not imputing to it a set of socially radical motives), I may appear in danger of repeating an increasingly common mistake in contemporary art histories. Too often we stuff complex practices into the sanctioned forms of the prevailing discourse. In doing so, we may elevate those practices, but we also risk disciplining their most plural, dangerous and telling aspects in the service of a framework that is relevant only insofar as it is available and shared, and thus deemed useful in conferring value. Today, insisting that a practice is 'radical' can be functionally indistinguishable from the flim-flam spouted by connoisseurs half a century ago.

To see my argument here within this frame would be to miscalculate what a discourse of wrongness, of activated and often corrupted space, actually has to offer us. In the introduction to his *Critique of Hegel's Philosophy of Right*, Marx articulated one of his neatest dialectics. Religion, he said, was 'the sigh of the oppressed creature, the heart of a heartless world, the soul of soulless conditions' (and thus 'the opium of the people').[31] He called for its inadequate consolations to be dispensed with, so as to lay bare the essence of social reality. In the intervening 175 years we have instead clung to religion – and begun, perhaps, to recognize something other than mere consolation in our reasons for clinging.

What we recognize is a drive to communal experience, to shared points of reference that might circumvent the reification of social reality – and more importantly, in the inevitable denial of this drive, a persistent sign of lack. This sign is the reverse side of comfort; it points to what is lost. As Bill Livant has it at the close of his piece on Hegel and Marx, 'the whole without a hole is really a part in drag trying to pass itself off as everything, which, come to think of it, isn't a bad definition of ideology.'[32] That is, the hole, the lack, the space where a space shouldn't be, is a kind of truth, and is perhaps all that lies between the mere posture of totality, and totality itself.

Affect is like this. That it exists and remains worthy of note is a guarantee of its inadequacy. It is often quiet and, as Fer notes of Wilding's sculpture, oblique. It can hardly be thought of as radical on its own. But it *points*.

1 Bill Livant, 'The Hole in Hegel's Bagel', in Bertell Ollman and Tony Smith (eds.), *Dialectics for the New Century*, New York 2008, p.199.

2 See Anthony Caro, 'The Master Sculptor', *The Observer*, 27 November 1960, p.21.

3 The class identities of the New Generation sculptors was touched upon in a recent essay by Toby Juliff. Toby Juliff, 'A New Generation of British Art: A Problem of Provincialism', *Australian and New Zealand Journal of Art* 18, no.1, 2018, pp.125–45 (pp.133–34).

4 The abbreviated history of institutional change outlined here is particularly informed by Jon Wood (ed.), *United Enemies: The Problem of Sculpture in Britain in the 1960s and 1970s*, Leeds 2011; and Jon Wood (ed.), *Making It: Sculpture in Britain, 1977–1986*, London 2015.

5 Clement Greenberg, 'The New Sculpture', in *Art and Culture*, Boston 1961, pp.139–45 (p.141).

6 Ibid., p.142.

7 See Fried's introduction to the catalogue of Caro's 1963 Whitechapel Gallery exhibition, *Anthony Caro*, London 1963.

8 Alex Potts, 'Anthony Caro, "Early One Morning"', in Penelope Curtis and Keith Wilson (eds.), *Modern British Sculpture*, London 2011, pp.176–85 (p.184).

9 Well-studied and beyond the scope of this essay, but far from irrelevant to the trends it describes, are the parallel debates around sculpture triggered by the emergence of minimalism in the United States. Of particular significance to the understanding that sculptures are also objects, and may be treated as such, are Donald Judd, 'Specific Objects', in William Seitz (ed.), *Contemporary Sculpture: Arts Yearbook 8*, New York 1965; and Robert Morris's four-part essay 'Notes on Sculpture', published in *Artforum* between 1966 and 1969.

10 Paul Moorhouse includes an especially useful discussion of the Table Pieces in '"The Forms of Things Unknown": Anthony Caro's Sculpture', in Moorhouse et al., *Anthony Caro*, exh. cat., Tate Britain, London 2005, pp.8–113 (pp.42–54).

11 Lynne Cooke, 'New Abstract Sculpture and its Sources', in Sandy Nairne and Nicholas Serota (eds.), *British Sculpture in the Twentieth Century*, London 1981, pp.167–83 (p.167).

12 Ibid.

13 Patrick Elliott, 'William Turnbull: A Consistent Way of Thinking', in David Sylvester and Patrick Elliott, *William Turnbull*, London 1995, pp.12–74 (p.57).

14 Michael Compton, 'A Developing Practice', in *Barry Flanagan: Sculpture*, London 1982, pp.17–28 (p.20).

15 From *Barry Flanagan: Exhibition of Small Works*, Liverpool 1974, quoted in *The Tate Gallery, 1972–4: Biennial Report and Illustrated Catalogue of Acquisitions*, London 1975, pp.133–34.

16 Tim Hilton, 'Less a Slave of Other People's Thinking', in *Barry Flanagan: Sculpture*, London 1982, pp.7–14 (p.11).

17 Williams's concept was first developed in texts including *Drama in Performance*, London 1954; *Preface to Film* (co-authored by Michael Orrom), London 1954; and *The Long Revolution*, London 1961.

18 Raymond Williams, *Marxism and Literature*, Oxford 1977, p.125, quoted in Terry Eagleton, *Ideology: An Introduction*, London 1991, p.48.

19 Charlotte Mullins, *RW: Rachel Whiteread*, London 2004, p.23.

20 Rosalind Krauss, 'X Marks the Spot', in Fiona Bradley et al., *Rachel Whiteread: Shedding Life*, exh. cat., Tate Liverpool, London 1996, pp.74–81 (p.76); Roland Barthes, *Camera Lucida*, trans. Richard Howard, London 1982, pp.92–93.

21 Krauss, in Bradley et al. 1996, p.80.

22 Briony Fer, 'Eyes Cast', in Gallagher and Donovan (eds.) 2017, pp.130–37 (p.137).

23 See Martin Heidegger, *Being and Time* [1927], trans. John McQuarrie and Edward Robinson, Oxford 1962, p.98.

24 Briony Fer, 'Zigzag: The Small Sculpture', in Jo Applin and Briony Fer, *Alison Wilding*, London 2018, pp.157–68 (pp.165–66).

25 Ibid., p.168.

26 Jo Applin, 'Beautiful, Deadly Things: The Sculpture of Alison Wilding', in Applin and Fer 2018, pp.9–154.

27 Alison Wilding, diary entry, 1976, quoted ibid., p.13.

28 Alfred Gell, 'Vogel's Net: Traps as Artworks and Artworks as Traps', *Journal of Material Culture* 1, no.1, 1996, pp.15–38 (p.27), quoted in Applin, in Applin and Fer 2018, p.153.

29 Marina Vaizey, 'Ideas into Art: Richard Long at the Lisson Gallery', *Financial Times*, 30 January 1970, p.3, quoted in Clarrie Wallis (ed.), *Stones, Clouds, Miles: A Richard Long Reader*, London 2016, pp.35–37 (p.36).

30 Richard Cork, 'Long's Stony Road to Success', *Evening Standard*, 1 February 1973, p.28, quoted in Wallis (ed.) 2016, pp.41–43 (p.43).

31 Karl Marx, *Critique of Hegel's Philosophy of Right*, ed. by Joseph O'Malley, trans. by Annette Jolin and Joseph O'Malley, Cambridge: Cambridge University Press, 1970, p.131.

32 Livant, in Ollman and Smith (eds.) 2008, p.199.

PLATES

Like Constantin Brancusi, whose studio he visited in Paris in the late 1940s, William Turnbull was interested in the subtle contrasts that emerge when materials are carefully stacked and played off each other. He was also a great admirer of Alberto Giacometti (whom he also visited at this time) and of Pablo Picasso, whose three-dimensional work, especially his plaster sculpture, was capturing the imagination of a generation of artists through the publication of *The Sculptures of Picasso* (1949), illustrated with compelling black-and-white photographs by Brassaï and and Dora Maar.

Sculpture (1956) at once draws on and departs from each of these artists, revealing the powerful extent to which the 34-year-old Turnbull had begun to find his own distinctive voice as a sculptor. It also highlights the ways in which he was successfully absorbing examples of earlier archaic and non-Western objects, creating a mixture of cultural and sculptural associations. This gives the work a striking openness and a direct manner of address: *Sculpture* is boldly front-facing, offering a compelling tandem image of horizontality and verticality in balance. There is also a combination of figurative and landscape associations at work here: person and place together. We might read the composition as a torso and arms, or two bodies, one standing and the other balanced on top. At the same time, looking closely at the corrugated and highly textured surfaces of the work, we might see the dips and furrows of fields and their patchwork landscape.

William Turnbull
Sculpture, 1956

Bronze, 147.3 × 38.1 × 124.5cm, edition of four

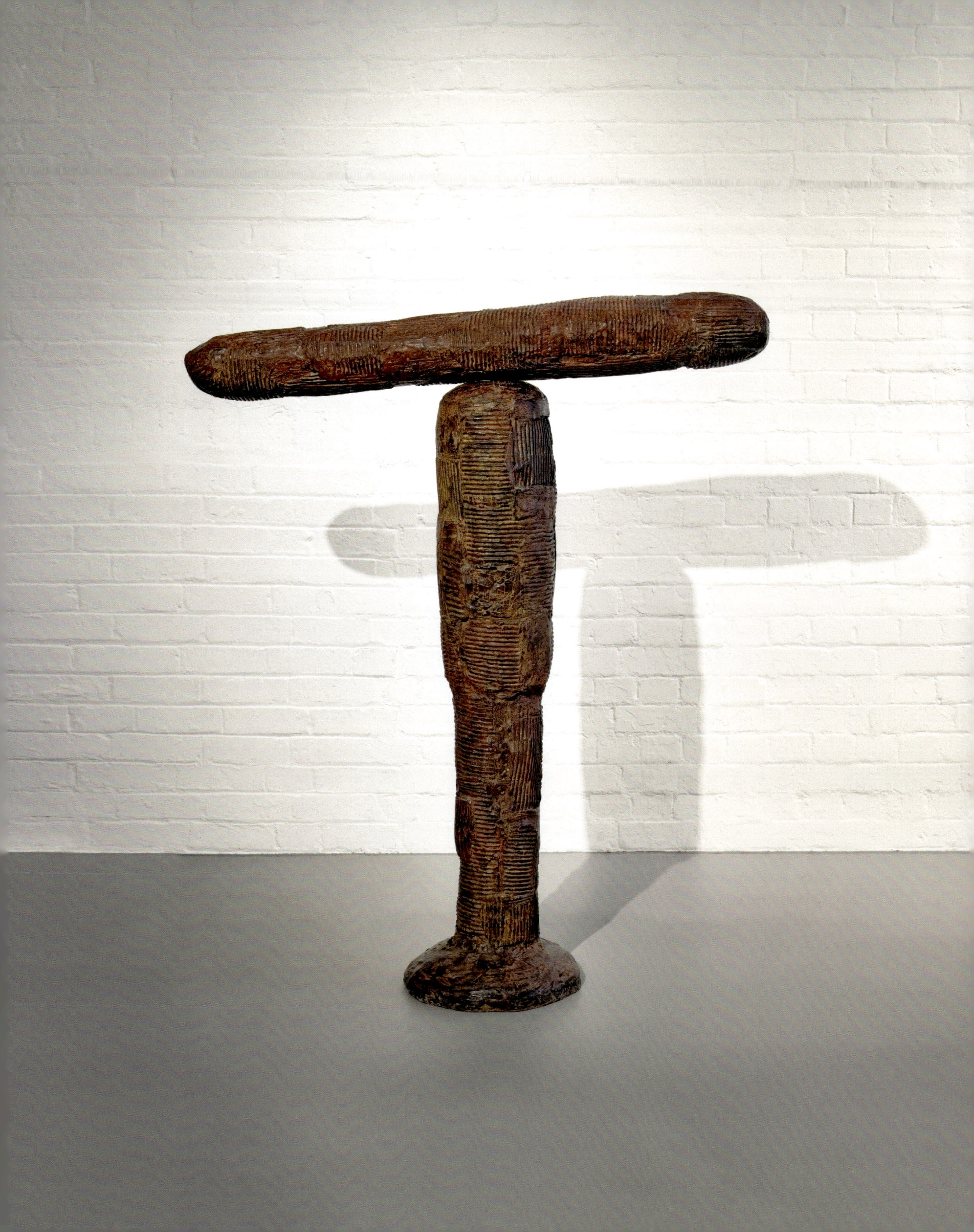

Barry Flanagan's *metal 2 '64* comprises sections of metal tubing and metal sheeting, jointed in the middle. The sculpture was part of a small series of works made while Flanagan was still a student, and at the time he exhibited it on the roof of the St Martin's School of Art building.

Part of the sculptural achievement and charm of the work lies in its bold use of space and the ways it harnesses and directs the spatial environment surrounding it. It is a highly gestural and calligraphic work, with grey painted lines, thick and thin, that evoke a snake-like, frenetic energy and unpredictability: a sculpture charged with potentiality and play. Poise, balance and asymmetry are central to this, as Hilary Gresty has commented: '*metal 2 '64* shows the intuitive application of unpredictable laws – a precarious balance is attained, the pipe being gently bent to display the possibilities of the material, the final form being off-set by the clean cut of the metal strip which is so positioned as to allow the plate to balance on an apex.'

This 1964 work also shows an interrogatory engagement with the possibilities of welded metal sculpture and, in turn, with the ideas of the St Martin's sculpture staff, which at the time included Phillip King, David Annesley, Isaac Witkin and Anthony Caro. The influence of concrete poetry is also present: that same year, Flanagan jointly started the concrete poetry magazine *Silâns*, and in *metal 2 '64* he adopts a liberated, spontaneous approach to the language and making of sculpture that similarly draws from this poetic sensibility.

Barry Flanagan
metal 2 '64, 1964

Mild painted steel, 91.4 × 426.7 × 76.2cm

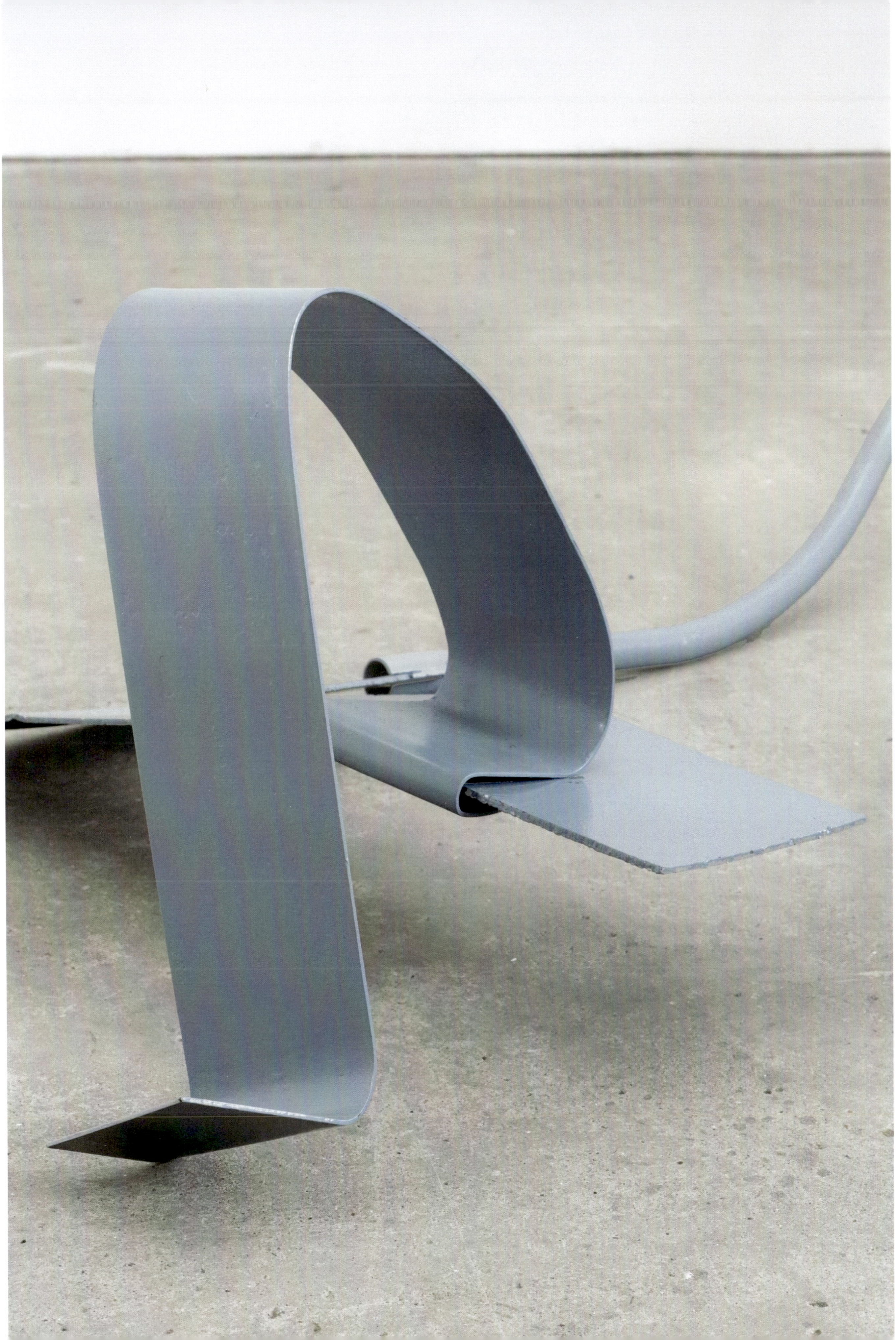

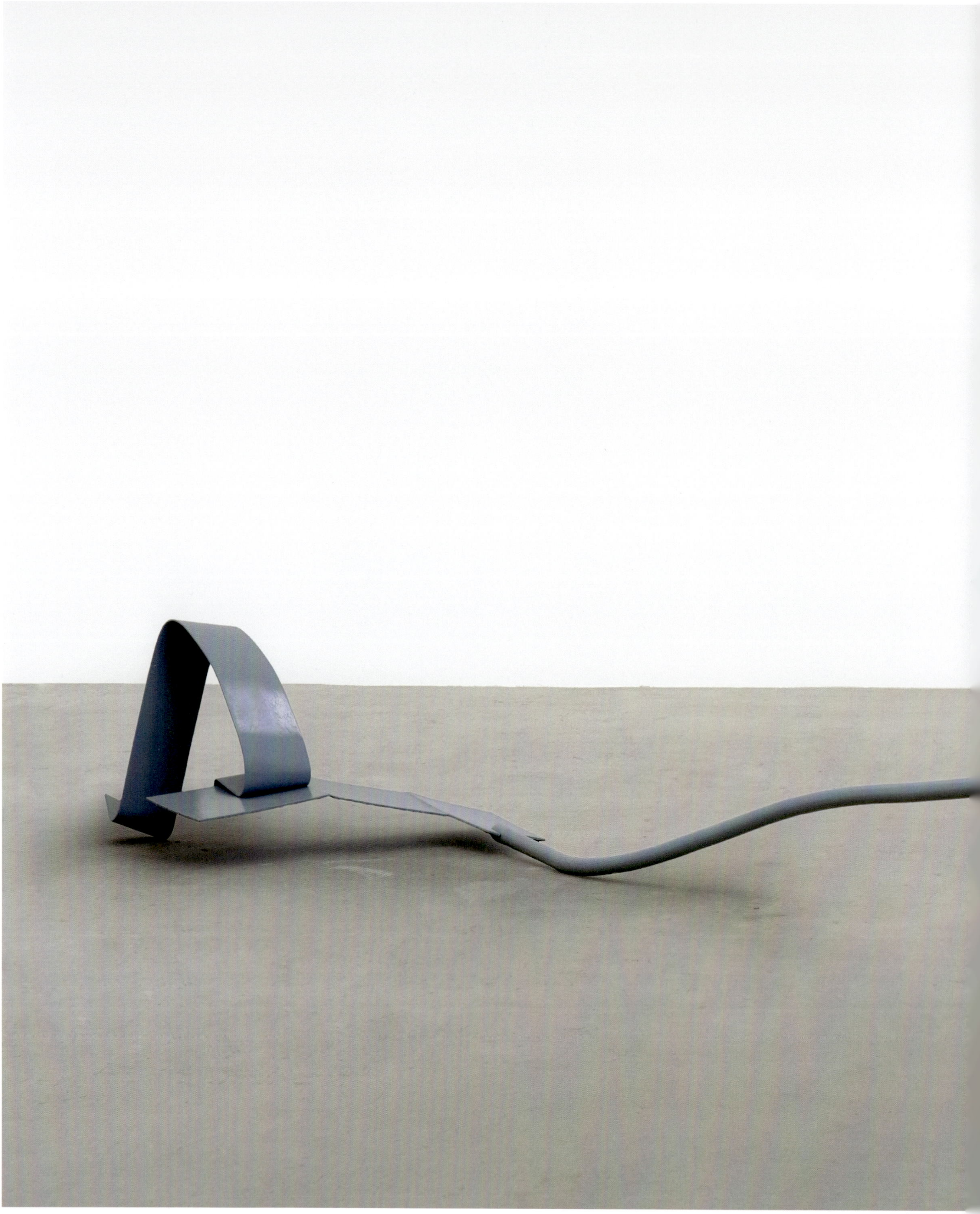

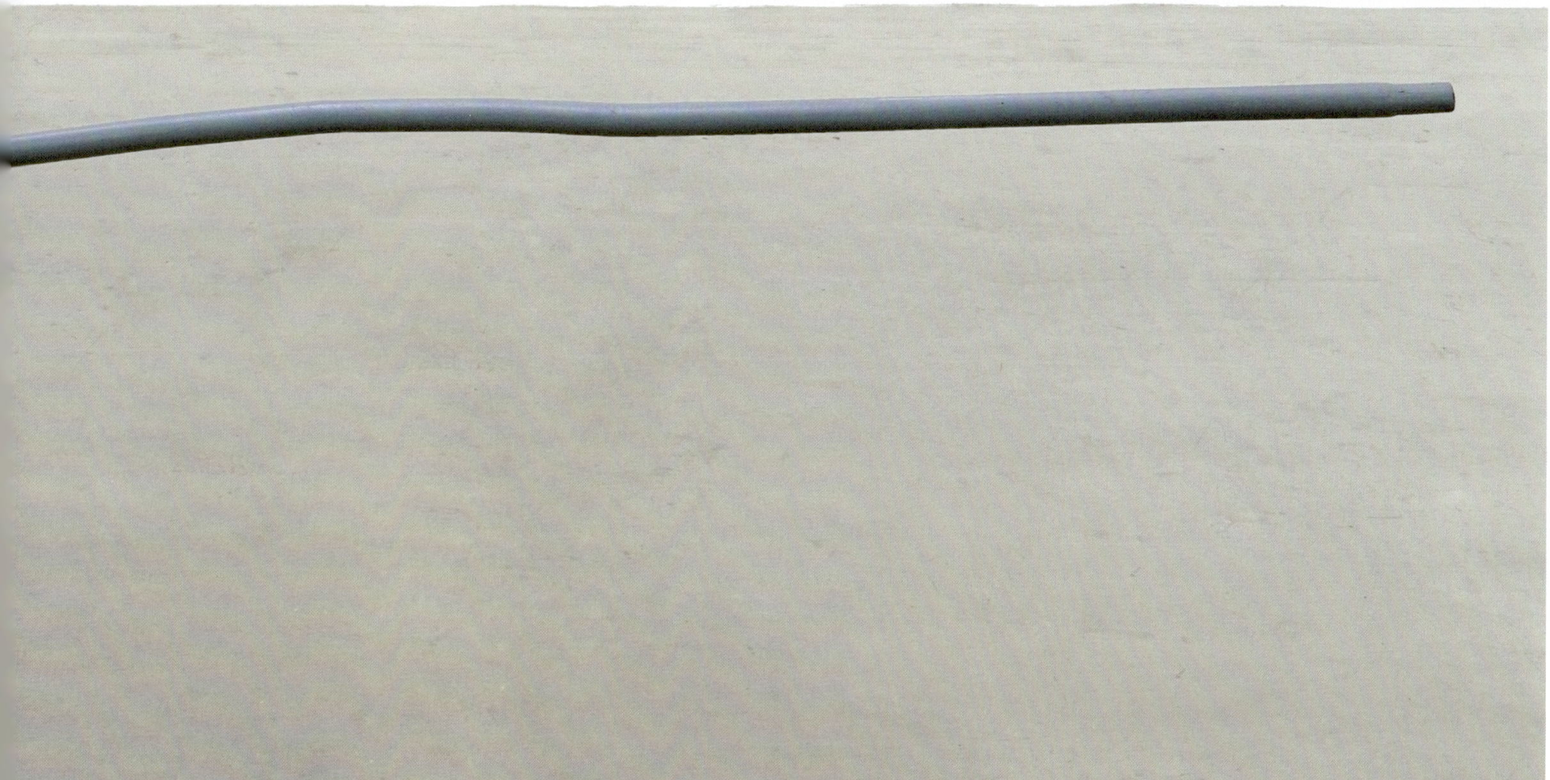

Like his famous *Early One Morning* (1962), in the Tate's collection, Anthony Caro's *Andy* is a red-painted, abstract welded steel sculpture – a type of work for which Caro became known in the 1960s and continues to be so today. However, by comparison to that earlier piece, horizontality has been exchanged for verticality and pillar-box red for a darker burgundy, as we are presented with a sculpture that operates as line, rather than volume, drawing in the air and activating the space around it. Two tall, thin rods stand upright, one leaning towards the other; they are fixed to the ends of shorter, thicker rods placed parallel on the ground, together providing the base support. *Andy* is concerned with verticality, asymmetry, the subtle distribution of weight and elegant poise. It is an exercise in balanced imbalance, with each section of metal subtly articulating the sculpture in space.

The work is refined, while also still powerful and present as a material object; qualities which are also found in works such as *Eyelit* (1965) and *Smoulder* (1965), made when the artist was in his early 40s. The mid-1960s was an important moment in Caro's career and coincided, in 1965, with the death of the American sculptor David Smith, who had been an inspiring figure for him. Caro had taken up a teaching position at Bennington College in Vermont between 1963 and 1964, where he became friends with the artist Jules Olitski, after whose wife Andrea this sculpture was named.

Anthony Caro
Andy, 1966

Steel painted red, 299.7 × 176.5 × 57.2cm

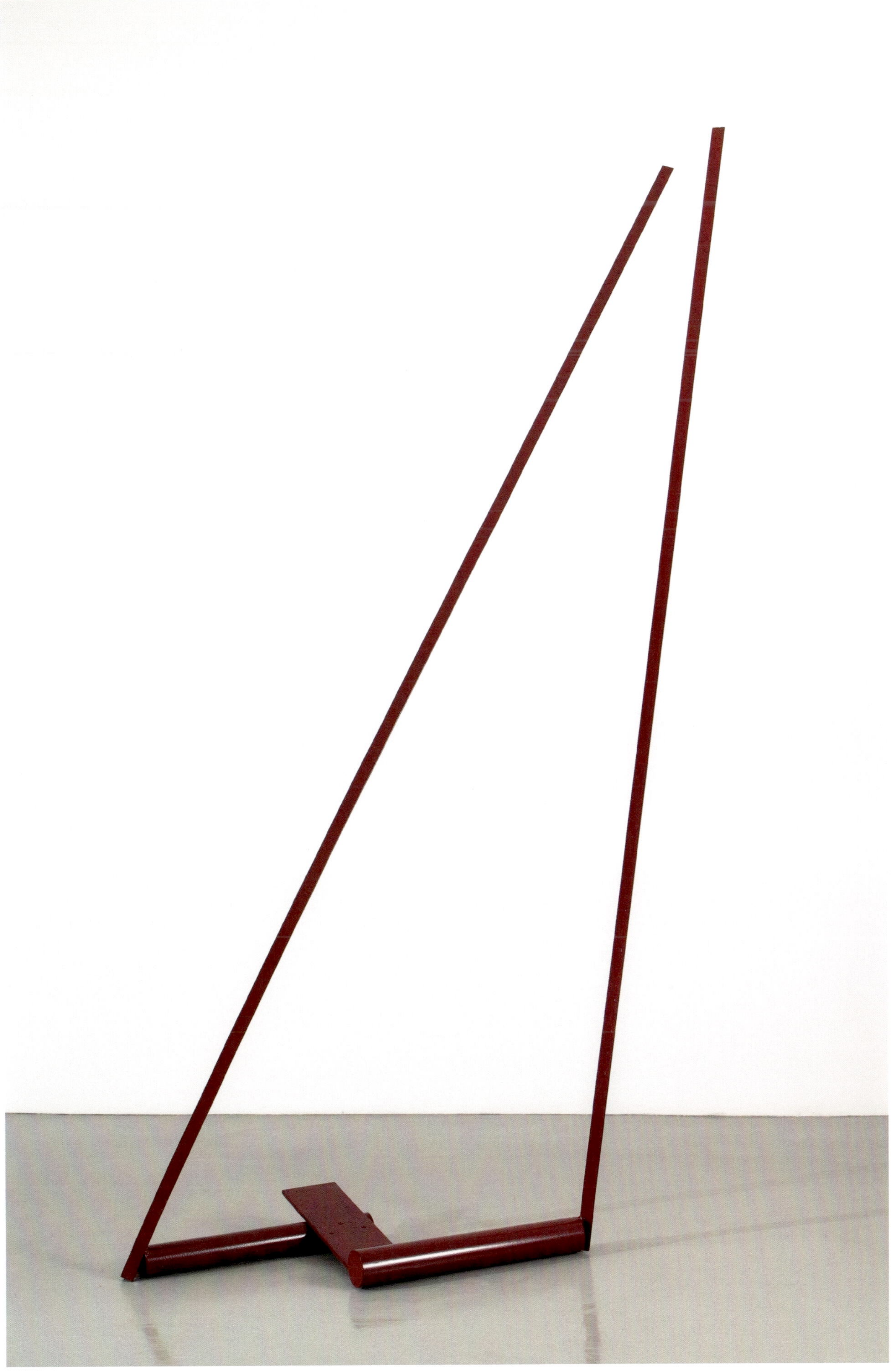

Since the 1960s, when Richard Long – then still a student at St Martin's School of Art – made his now famous *A Line Made by Walking* (1967), the artist has made works that are concerned with the human experience of landscape and how it is articulated. His work may involve walks, maps, drawings, texts, photographs and sculptures, these latter comprising natural material objects such as rocks, stones and pebbles, bringing the direct and compelling materiality of their particular environments with them while at the same time forming new compositions and juxtapositions in the space of the gallery or museum, where visitors themselves can walk around the works.

Circles, as ancient symbols carrying immediate and timeless power, have an important role in Long's work. *Red Slate Circle* (1980) comprises 61 stones, each placed on its flattest, most stable side, with no one stone touching another. The space between the stones becomes an active part of the work through the dialogue created between solid and void. Both stones and circle have a human, bodily scale that highlights the artist's personal physical involvement in the work.

In the accompanying hand-written certificate Long explains that the stones must be placed randomly and at an even density inside a circle measuring eight feet in diameter. The red slate was quarried in New York State and the subtle variations in the colour and pattern of the stones mean that no two circles, once assembled, will be alike. There are two *Red Slate Circles* in public collections: *Red Slate Circle* (1980) in the Guggenheim, New York, and *Red Slate Circle* (1988) in the Tate, London.

Richard Long
Red Slate Circle, 1980

Red slate – 61 pieces, diameter: 243.8cm

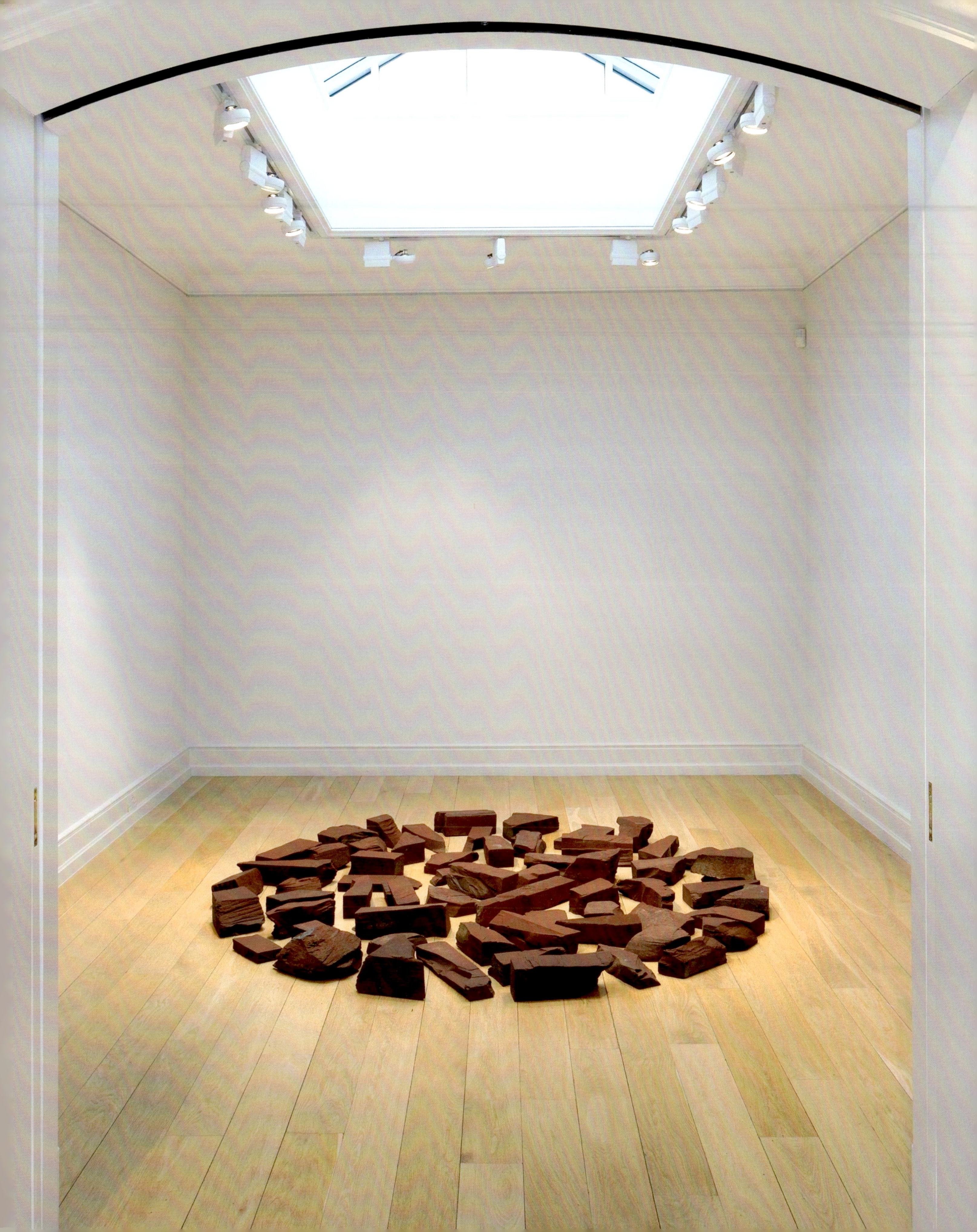

The appearance and disappearance of Rachel Whiteread's cast concrete *House* (1993–94) brought to national and international attention the power of contemporary sculpture to deal with real spaces as much as real people and provoking questions about private and public space.

Whiteread has become known for her haunting cast plaster, concrete and rubber sculptures in which the empty spaces around or within objects are made solid, the passing of time traced and their relationship to the human body activated. *Garage* (2005) is one such sculpture: plaster casts of cardboard boxes piled upon and under a painted steel and wood table. Like the domestic garages that often house them, cardboard boxes are storage spaces, small units typically stuffed with personal belongings and stacked out of sight. Plaster, with its evocation of the body and the skeletal, was perhaps chosen for the tenderness and vulnerability it brings to these containers. *Garage* evokes this compelling domestic context, creating a *mise en abyme*-like box-within-a-box and presenting abstracted yet characteristic forms that are at once full and empty, present and absent.

Rachel Whiteread
Garage, 2005

Plaster, painted steel and laminated wood, 113 × 124.5 × 69.2cm

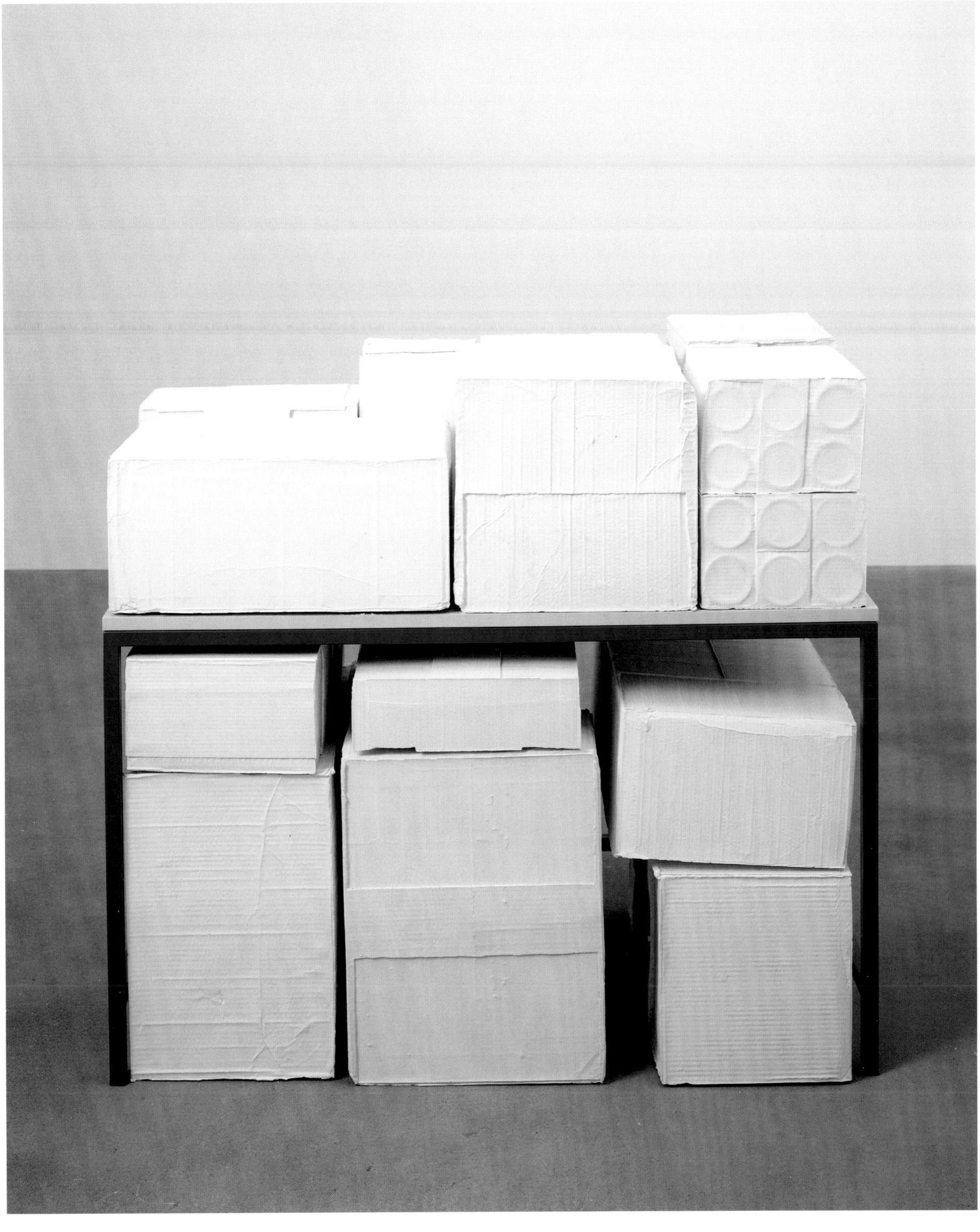

Alison Wilding's *In a Dark Wood* (2012) is a large sculpture made of strips of reclaimed laminated iroko, a tough and durable hardwood often used for flooring, panelling and cabinetmaking, coupled with a number of acrylic spheres, which are lodged within.

The sculpture is part of a larger body of monocoque works – in which skin and structure inextricably coincide – that began in 1990 with *Inland*. These works have all been carefully built up, layer upon layer, out of sections of interlocking mirrored stainless steel or translucent PVC and acrylic. *In a Dark Wood* is a fascinating departure from these earlier works, as Wilding here explores the different qualities and visual effects of wood. Through discussion with Adam Kershaw, who fabricated the work, Wilding introduced a degree of randomness in contrast to the strict geometry of previous monocoque sculptures.

In a Dark Wood gives us two intersecting and enmeshed forms, which might suggest both the arboreal and anthropomorphic. The title is drawn from the beginning of the first Canto of the 'Inferno' of Dante's *Divine Comedy*: 'In the middle of our life's journey, I found myself in a dark wood, where the direct way was lost.'

Alison Wilding
In a Dark Wood, 2012

Reclaimed laminated iroko and acrylic, 210 × 370 × 217cm

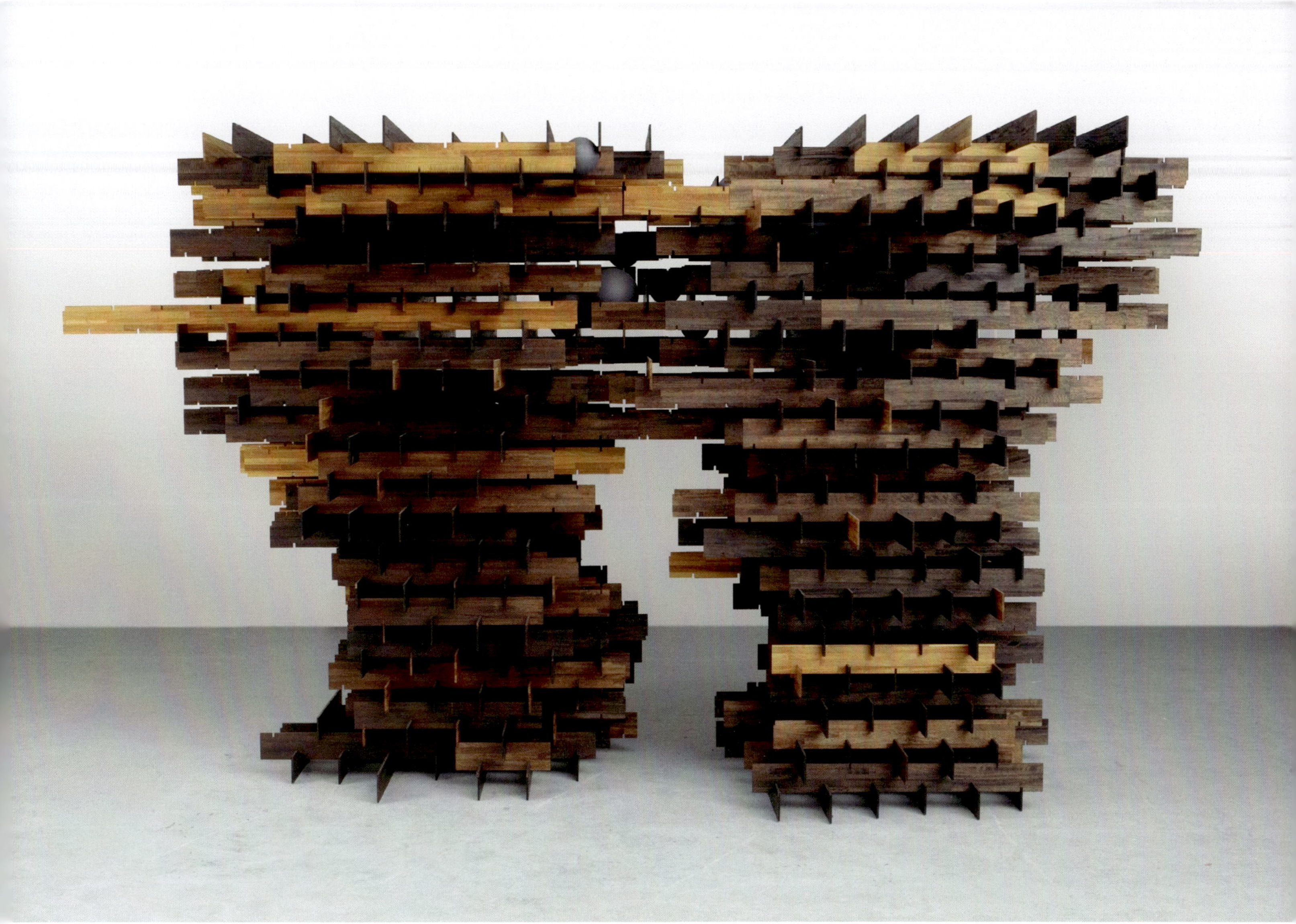

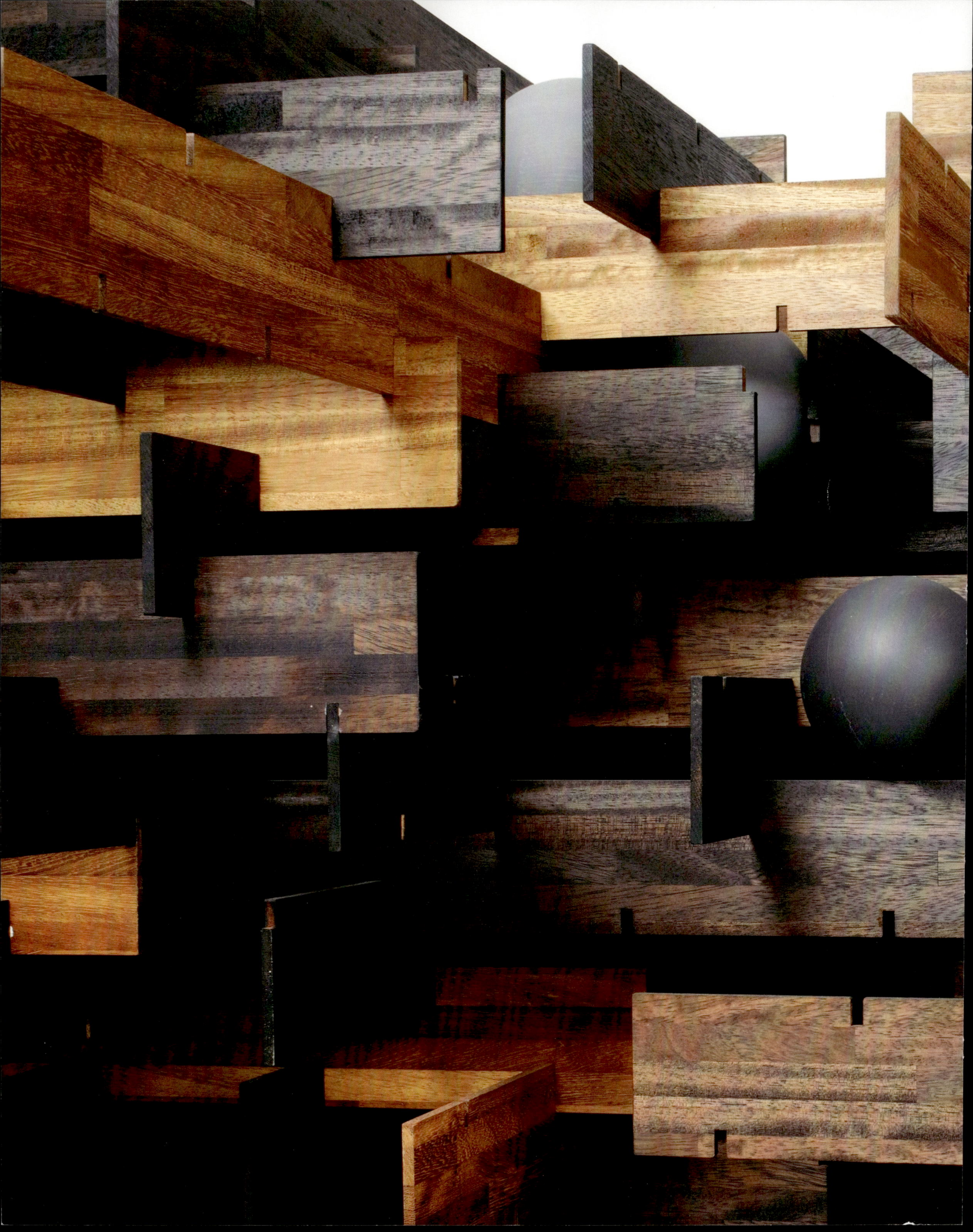

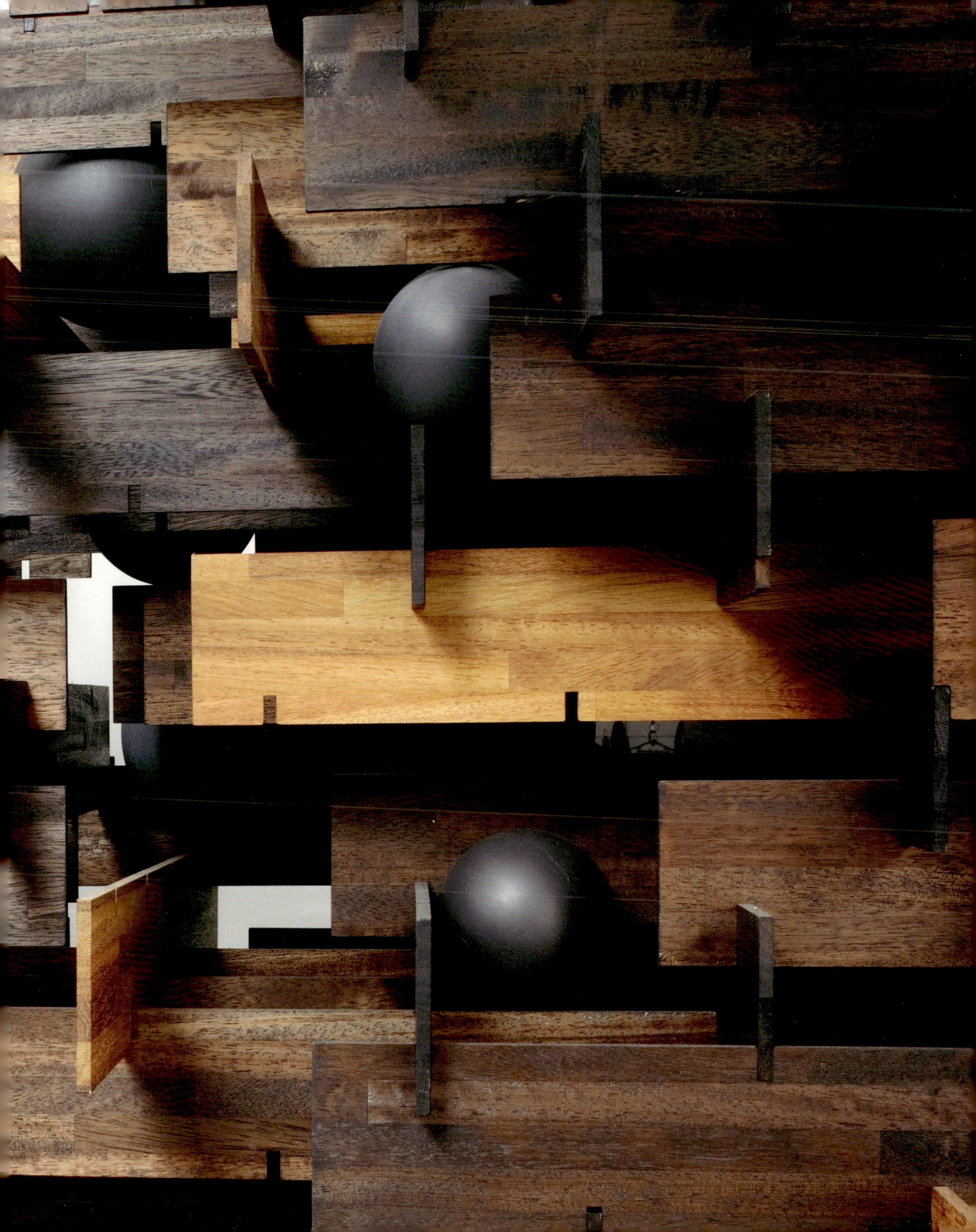

SELECT BIBLIOGRAPHY

This bibliography represents a limited selection of the best writing available on the sculptors in this exhibition, as well as major surveys, contextual studies and texts of particular historical importance to the period.

GENERAL

Britannica: Trente ans de sculpture, Le Havre: Musée des Beaux-Arts, 1988.
Causey, Andrew, *Sculpture since 1945*, Oxford: Oxford University Press, 1998.
Cork, Richard, *New Spirit, New Sculpture, New Money: Art in the 1980s*, New Haven and London: Yale University Press, 2003.
Curtis, Penelope and Wilson, Keith (eds.), *Modern British Sculpture*, London: Royal Academy of Arts, 2011.
Harrison, Charles, *Charles Harrison: Looking Back*, London: Ridinghouse, 2011.
Krauss, Rosalind, *Passages in Modern Sculpture*, New York: Viking Press, 1977.
Mellor, David, *The Sixties Art Scene in London*, London: Phaidon, 1993.
Nairne, Sandy and Serota, Nicholas (eds.), *British Sculpture in the Twentieth Century*, London: Whitechapel Art Gallery, 1981.
Neff, Terry (ed.), *A Quiet Revolution: British Sculpture since 1965*, New York and London: Thames and Hudson, 1987.
Portelli, Guy, *Modern British Sculpture*, Atglen: Schiffer Publishing Ltd., 2005.
Potts, Alex, *The Sculptural Imagination: Figurative, Modernist, Minimalist*, New Haven and London: Yale University Press, 2000.
Rowell, Margit (ed.), *Qu'est-ce que la sculpture moderne?*, Paris: Centre Georges Pompidou, 1986.
Seymour, Anne et al., *The New Art*, London: Arts Council of Great Britain, 1972.
Stephens, Chris and Bindman, David (ed.), *The History of British Art, Vol.3: 1870–Now*, London: Tate Publishing Ltd. and New Haven: Yale University Press, 2008.
Szeemann, Harald (ed.), *Live in Your Head: When Attitudes Become Form (Works–Concepts–Processes–Situations–Information)*, Bern: Kunsthalle Bern, 1969.
Biggs, Lewis, Chambers, Ian, Cooke, Lynne, Francis, Richard, Harrison, Charles and Kunz, Martin, *Starlit Waters, British Sculpture: An International Art 1968–1988*, Liverpool: Tate Gallery, 1988.
Tiberghien, Gilles A., *Land Art*, Paris: Éditions Carré, 1995.
Windsor, Alan, *British Sculptors of the Twentieth Century*, Farnham: Ashgate, 2003.
Wood, Jon (ed.), *Making It: Sculpture in Britain 1977–1986*, London: Hayward Publishing 2015.
— *United Enemies: The Problem of Sculpture in Britain in the 1960s and 1970s*, Leeds: Henry Moore Institute, 2011.
Wood, Jon, Hulks, David and Potts, Alex (eds.), *Modern Sculpture Reader*, Leeds: Henry Moore Institute, 2007.

ANTHONY CARO

Fenton, Terry, *Anthony Caro*, London: Thames and Hudson, 1986.
Fried, Michael, *Anthony Caro*, London: Whitechapel Gallery, 1963.
Hilton, Tim, *Anthony Caro: Sculpture 1969–84*, London: Serpentine Gallery, 1984.
Krauss, Rosalind, 'How Paradigmatic is Anthony Caro?', *Art in America*, September–October 1975, pp.80–83.
Moorhouse, Paul (ed.), *Anthony Caro*, London: Tate Publishing, 2005.
Rubin, William, *Anthony Caro*, New York: Museum of Modern Art and London: Thames & Hudson, 1975.
Waldman, Diane, *Anthony Caro*, Oxford: Phaidon Press, 1982.

BARRY FLANAGAN

Baro, Gene, 'Animal, Vegetable and Mineral', *Art and Artists* 1, no.6, September 1966, p.63.
— in discussion with Barry Flanagan, 'Sculpture Made Visible', *Studio International* 178, no.915, October 1969, p.124.
Barry Flanagan Object Sculptures, Krefeld: Museum Haus Lange, 1969.
Celant, Germano, *Arte Povera*, New York: Praeger, 1969.
Compton, Michael and Hilton, Tim, *Barry Flanagan: Sculpture*, London: British Council, 1982.
Harrison, Charles, 'Barry Flanagan's Sculpture', *Studio International* 175, no.900, May 1968, p.266.
Juncosa, Enrique, Thompson, Jon, Gleadowe, Teresa, Pringle, Alexandra and Rudrum, Clarrie, *Barry Flanagan*, Madrid: Fundación "la Caixa", 1993.
Juncosa, Enrique (ed.), *Barry Flanagan Sculpture 1965–2005*, Dublin: Irish Museum of Modern Art, 2006, p.59.
Melvin, Jo, *Barry Flanagan: works 1966–2008*, London: Waddington Galleries, 2010.
Wallis, Clarrie and Wilson, Andrew (eds.), *Barry Flanagan: early works, 1965–1982*, London: Tate Publishing, 2011.

RICHARD LONG

Compton, Michael, *Some Notes on the Work of Richard Long*, London: British Council, 1976.

Fuchs, R.H., *Richard Long*, London and New York: Thames and Hudson and the Solomon R. Guggenheim Museum, 1986.

Long, Richard, Seymour, Anne, Moorhouse, Paul and Hooker, Denise, *Richard Long: Walking the Line*, London: Thames & Hudson, 2002.

Long, Richard, Seymour, Anne and Fulton, Hamish, *Richard Long: Walking in Circles*, London: South Bank Centre, 1991.

Wallis, Clarrie (ed.), *Richard Long: Heaven and Earth*, London: Tate Publishing, 2009.

— *Stones, Clouds, Miles: A Richard Long Reader*, London: Ridinghouse, 2016.

WILLIAM TURNBULL

Alloway, Lawrence, 'The sculpture and painting of William Turnbull', *Art International* 5, no.1, 1st February 1961, pp.46–52.

Davidson, Amanda A., *The Sculpture of William Turnbull*, Much Hadham: Henry Moore Foundation; Aldershot: Lund Humphries, 2005.

Elliott, Patrick and Sylvester, David, *William Turnbull: Sculptures and Paintings*, London: Merrell Holberton and Serpentine Gallery, 1995.

Mellor, David, 'Existentialism and post-war British art', in Frances Morris (ed.), *Paris Post War: Art & Existentialism 1945–55*, London: Tate Gallery, 1993, pp.53–63.

Morphet, Richard, *William Turnbull: Sculpture and Painting*, London: Tate Gallery Publications, 1973.

Ngui, Caroline, 'Sculpture with a Presence', *Straits Times*, 19th September 1984.

William Turnbull: Sculpture and Paintings, London: Waddington Galleries, 1998.

William Turnbull: Beyond Time, London: Waddington Galleries, 2010.

RACHEL WHITEREAD

Batchelor, David, *Rachel Whiteread: Plaster Sculptures*, London and New York: Karsten Schubert Ltd. and Luhring Augustine Gallery, 1993.

Colomina, Beatriz, Dennison, Lisa, Homes, A.M. and Houser, Craig, *Rachel Whiteread: Transient Spaces*, Ostfildern: Hatje Cantz, 2001.

Debbaut, Jan (ed.), *Rachel Whiteread: Sculptures*, Eindhoven: Stedelijk Van Abbemuseum, 1993.

Lingwood, James (ed/), *House*, London: Phaidon, 1995.

Gallagher, Anne (ed.), *Rachel Whiteread: British Pavilion, XLVII Venice Biennale*, London: British Council, 1997.

Gallagher, Anne and Donovan, Molly (eds.), *Rachel Whiteread*, London: Tate Publishing, 2017.

Krauss, Rosalind, Marí, Bartomeu, Morgan, Stuart, and Tarantino, Michael, *Rachel Whiteread: Shedding Life*, London: Tate Gallery Publishing, 1996.

Mullins, Charlotte, *RW: Rachel Whiteread*, rev. edn, London: Tate Publishing, (2004) 2017.

Townsend, Chris (ed.), *The Art of Rachel Whiteread*, London: Thames & Hudson, 2004.

ALISON WILDING

Applin, Jo, and Fer, Briony, *Alison Wilding*, London: Lund Humphries and Ridinghouse, 2018.

Collins, Judy, Mengham, Rod and Porrit, Sam, *Alison Wilding: Tracking*, London: Ridinghouse, 2008.

Curtis, Penelope (ed.), *Alison Wilding Contract*, Halifax and Leeds: Dean Clough and the Henry Moore Foundation, 2000.

Curtis, Penelope, Moszynska, Anna, Wilding, Alison and Juliá, Carmen, *Alison Wilding: Vanish & Detail*, London: Ridinghouse, 2014.

Curtis, Penelope (ed.), *Alison Wilding: Immersion/Exposure*, Liverpool: Tate Gallery, 1991.

PHOTO CREDITS

© Alison Wilding: pp.27 (photo: the artist), 47–49 (photos: Peter White)

© Anthony Caro. Courtesy of Barford Sculptures Ltd: pp.4, 16 and 41

© Estate of Barry Flanagan: pp.37–39 (photos: David Ward)

© Phillip King. Courtesy the artist and Thomas Dane Gallery: p.21

© Rachel Whiteread 2019: pp.25 and 45 (photo: courtesy of Gagosian)

© Richard Long. All Rights Reserved, DACS 2019: pp.29 (photo: courtesy of the National Galleries of Scotland), 43 (photo: courtesy of akg-images)

© Richard Serra. Courtesy of the San Francisco Museum of Modern Art and the studio of Richard Serra: p.26 (photo: Saul Rosenfield)

© Tate, London 2019: p.20

© William Turnbull. All Rights Reserved, DACS 2019, pp. 19 (photo: courtesy of Waddington Custcot) and 35

Published in 2019 by Ridinghouse

on the occasion of the exhibition
Dialectical Materialism: Aspects of British Sculpture Since the 1960s
at Karsten Schubert
1 Park Village East,
London NW1 7PX
28 September–6 October 2019

Ridinghouse
46 Lexington Street
London W1F OLP
United Kingdom
ridinghouse.co.uk

Distributed in the UK and Europe by
Cornerhouse Publications
c/o Home
2 Tony Wilson Place
Manchester M15 4FN
United Kingdom
cornerhousepublications.org

Distributed in the United States and Canada by
ARTBOOK | D.A.P.
75 Broad Street, Suite 630
New York, New York 10004
artbook.com

British Library Cataloguing-in-Publication Data
A full catalogue record of this book is available from the British Library.

ISBN 978 1 909932 54 8

Ridinghouse Publisher: Sophie Kullmann
Edited by Aimee Selby and Sophie Kullmann

Designed by Mark Thomson

Printed in Belgium by die Keure

Ridinghouse